IRELAND
THROUGH
BIRDS

D1343160

IRELAND THROUGH BIRDS

Journeys in Search of a Wild Nation

CONOR W. O'BRIEN

MERRION
PRESS

First published in 2019 by
Merrion Press
An imprint of Irish Academic Press
10 George's Street
Newbridge
Co. Kildare
Ireland
www.merrionpress.ie

9781785373053 (Paper)
9781785373060 (Kindle)
9781785373077 (Epub)
9781785373084 (PDF)

British Library Cataloguing in Publication Data
An entry can be found on request

Library of Congress Cataloging in Publication Data
An entry can be found on request

Typeset in Sabon LT Std 11.5/15 pt

Jacket design by River Design

All illustrations courtesy of the Royal Society for the
Protection of Birds/Mike Langman (rspb-images.com)

CONTENTS

For Ma, Da and Neil.

Thanks also to Mark for all his help
on my Wicklow journeys.

INTRODUCTION

A Nation and its Birds

*By retaining one's childhood love of such things as
trees, rivers, butterflies ... one makes a peaceful and
decent future a little more probable*

— George Orwell

Above, the pale March sky is flecked with clouds.
Beneath the bridge I stand on, the aqua green water
of the Leitrim River glistens. Gorse bushes coming into
bloom spring from its banks. They add a rich yellow to
the scene. The scent of the gorse, like coconut, lingers on
the breeze. I expect a jogger to come pounding across the
rusty iron bridge at any second. But if only for a moment,
there's not a soul to be seen.

During blissful vignettes like this, I like to close my
eyes, and sink into the other senses. As I do so, the colourful
palette before me wipes to crimson, and I let my mind
drift to the sounds of the scene. I unplug my headphones,
and flick my phone to silent. A faint rustle of the breeze
resonates. From the nearby coast, the cry of a herring gull
echoes. Much closer, a stonechat – they're never far from
gorse – gives off its distinctive *weet-chat*, like a whistle
followed by two stones being smacked together. Were it
not for the distant purr of a helicopter, there'd be no man-
made noise whatsoever. I could be in an Ireland before (or

after) man, instead of just ten minutes from my front door. Total immersion in nature.

It's one of my favourite things to do with my spare time. In an age of constant beeps, by-the-minute updates, and a never-ending cavalcade of scandals and developments we have to stay abreast of, remaining attuned with nature, with organic sights and sounds, is a vital tonic for the soul. Many a stressful day or week, stuck in front of a computer or in a stuffy meeting room, has been salvaged or soothed by scenes like this. What makes it all the better is the company of creatures, great and small, adding dashes of movement to the portrait around me.

Of particular interest to me are the birds. I've been fascinated by birds since I was a child, when I crafted all manner of feeding contraptions from cardboard to tempt them to our back garden. Over time, my kit has grown more sophisticated, and my horizons have broadened beyond backyard visitors (not that they should ever be overlooked). When I'm at my desk, I often find myself yearning to be at an estuary or up a hill somewhere, looking for birds. They give you an excuse to get outdoors. I find myself poring through reports of the latest sightings, turning over logistics in my mind: where I'm going, how to get there, and what I hope to see when I arrive.

And yet, through all my excursions to wetlands, woods and cliffs near and far, there are still Irish species that have eluded me. Among them are the birds I will be covering in these pages; twelve species, each special in their own way. They include top predators of day and night; migrants who cross continents to be here; sea-going pirates; underhanded nest parasites; songsters of the high mountains; and ingenious forest dwellers – all of them beautifully adapted to vastly different lifestyles. In so doing, some of them have earned their way into Irish lore, a note in a rich ballad whose music I'll strive to unwind.

I like to think it's no surprise they've eluded me for so long. The twelve birds I will focus my search on for this book are not the easiest to see. Most of them are shy and wary. Some are highly localised; some need very specific conditions in which to flourish, conditions now found in only a few protected pockets across Ireland. Some are endangered – and still declining. And with some, it's just a matter of being in the right place at the right time.

Places. This will be a book about birds. But it will also be a book about *places*. Now, when we can travel the world with ease, the treasures on our own backdoor can so often be taken for granted.

I'm proof of this. I've been to more than a dozen countries across three continents. And yet I've never wound my way through the scree-covered mountains of Kerry, seen the Connemara countryside in all its summer glory or hiked the barren islands of Donegal. This book is my attempt to rectify that, to get to know my country, its landscapes, its history and its birds that little bit better. With luck I can inspire you to explore and savour the wild spaces around you as well.

It's not just new places I'll be striving to see. Of equal import will be seeing old locations, scenes from a childhood long gone, and what creatures my eyes and ears (that bit more attuned to nature) can now discern there. For the beauty of birding is that you don't always have to go far to find wonders. Species you've never seen before can suddenly turn up in your own county, your own town, your own patch. Or maybe they were there all along, evading your detection.

Modernity suits some birds, but not others. Many of the birds that will be covered in this book have made their homes in areas people have barely touched – remote islands, rugged valleys and slopes. Others still find their shelter amid the desolation left by humans in retreat (abandoned farm buildings and weather-beaten outhouses so often make ideal nest sites) or in the few places where traditional lifestyles still hold sway. It's also, therefore, no surprise that some of the locations I'll have to travel to (with a few notable exceptions, such as Dublin's Phoenix Park) are about as far from the major population centres as it's possible to be in Ireland. It's a journey that will take me to all four provinces, across barriers of language, culture and history, and through virtually every habitat type this island has to offer.

Places are a reflection of their history, much as you are the person your experiences have moulded you into. This is something I've always loved about Ireland, and about being Irish. With few exceptions, it's hard not to get a feel for history everywhere you go. In some places, it seems to hang in the air around you. So it's instructive to me to see how these birds fit in amongst all this, their thread weaving through the rich tapestry that makes up our changing landscapes. Their fate is so often reflected in the human history of the regions they call home.

I'm not naïve enough to think that showing up in the right spot at the right time entitles me to tick every bird off this list. Birdwatching is rarely an exact science. You can traverse the country to show up at the right spot in the right season, only for your quarry to manifest back where you started from. Nature rarely conforms to the vanities of man. That's one of its great allures. Plenty of times I've found myself wondering why I left a warm bed on a cold winter's morning to go exploring a windswept wetland or forest pelted with rain. But, if you're treated to a glimpse of a new or elusive species, however brief, you forget any hardship that led you to it.

One thing I've learned from my birdwatching sojourns near and far is that birds are vessels for a kind of lasting happiness that can be hard to find in other avenues of life. Nights out are great fun in the moment, but the memories soon fade with sobriety. The joy of immersing yourself in nature, of finding a new or rare bird, never leaves you. You can still recall every sensation months or years later.

Birdwatching harkens back to the primal state of man: stalking prey, zeroing in on a distant target, trying to get close without inciting alarm. It is perhaps this ancestral desire to track and discover that makes it so compelling. Only now, the hunt doesn't end in blood. An appreciation of the bird in its environs is reward enough, a photo perhaps the only trophy.

In searching for birds rarer now than they once were, perhaps there is some way to arrest the ancestral disconnect that so plagues us in a world obsessed with the here and now. In the croak of the corncrake or the shriek of the barn owl, I'll be hearing sounds much more common generations ago; an aural window into a time now gone, like a song never committed to paper.

There will be frustrations. There will be failures. But it's not all about finding a target at the expense of everything else. It's a journey to be enjoyed for its own sake.

Birds have seen better days in Ireland. While awareness of their plight is at an all-time high, and sympathy strong, many species are now in retreat. Of the twelve I cover in this book, all but one (the jay) are in some degree of trouble in Ireland (though the great skua is a nascent breeder here). Five of them (the barn owl, the grey partridge, the red grouse, the corncrake and the ring ouzel) are red listed by Birdwatch Ireland, the highest category of conservation concern.

The plight of the birds I will cover in this book is compounded by a few themes they share in common. Among them are their nesting habits. Of the twelve, only the jack snipe doesn't breed in Ireland. Of the eleven that do, most nest on the ground. In a country where more and more of our wilderness is chewed up by farming, urbanisation or just under foot, this leaves them acutely vulnerable.

The erosion of montane habits and onset of mechanised farming in particular have taken a heavy toll. This is not to denigrate farmers, living or dead. As someone with strong rural roots, it's likely my own forebears contributed, in their ignorance, to some of the changes that have afflicted Ireland's birds. They were only doing what they knew to be right, trying their best to eke prosperity from the land. Now, with the knowledge we have, it's our duty to help balance the needs of farmer and bird to ensure both have a home in twenty-first-century Ireland.

We relish our image as a green island replete with the wonders of nature. In truth, the pockets of wilderness we have left are still receding, and many of them are deeply degraded. Our seas and rivers are far from the wellsprings of purity they once were. Even the enclaves of forest that still cling to hillsides across the country are so often comprised of ecological aliens: trees that belong half the world away, which would not be here if not for the profit of man. You can feel this as you walk among them; they're dead zones, draining the soil of its fecundity as their canopies strangle the sunlight needed to sustain an undergrowth.

Our landscapes have also largely been shorn of the large mammals that once called them home. Wild boar, wolves and bears have all gone. Even the cherished red deer we have left have largely been sullied by the genes of the invasive sika.

This should make us cherish the avifauna, the birds we have left, all the more. The abundance of birds we have makes them an ideal conduit to the natural world, the space beyond beeps, car engines and keyboard strokes. For every species of mammal in Ireland (on both land and sea) at least five species of bird have been recorded here. This diversity is what guarantees a unique experience almost every time you set off birding. Even at my most well-explored spots I still encounter rarities; birds blown off course, or perhaps stopping over on a deliberate detour, stocking up on food before resuming a long migration north or south.

Ireland is beautifully positioned in this regard – at all times of year. Like an island trading post growing rich on the flow of silks and gold from one continent to another, we're perfectly situated for a host of seasonal birds on their biannual journeys from Eurasia to Africa. Our avifauna changes complexion throughout the year, from the vast hosts of ducks and waders we welcome each winter to the magnificent seabird colonies that fill our cliffs in summer. Among these seasonal stopovers are some of the birds I will search for in this book. Even some resident birds, like the merlin and hen harrier, change their habits with the seasons, descending to the lowlands where they can be more easily seen.

Because of this, a journey in search of birds lets you relish Ireland throughout the year. My travels will see me looking for birds in all shades of weather. Easy are the pleasures of a sun-drenched summer day. But there is a more esoteric beauty to be had in a landscape dripping from winter rain, darkened by brooding clouds above.

As a boy I would go on adventures looking for a particular bird, sometimes with success, very often without. Like many people, I fell more out of love with the natural world as a teenager, when other passions (music, football, females) bloomed, only to return to it with a new vigour as an adult.

Now, my desire to uncover new, unseen inhabitants of wild spaces is stronger than ever. This book is, in a way, the fulfilment of boyhood vision. But with the onset of adulthood, you can indulge childhood enthusiasms to a degree never before possible. My previous expeditions were limited to the forest behind my house and grandparents' gardens. Now I have the whole of Ireland laid out in front of me, ready to explore one valley, forest or country road at a time.

MERLIN

Dundalk

The chase is on. The tranquillity of the wetland is shattered as a cloud of starlings and finches bursts from the grass, and writhes in rapid undulation like a great airborne mollusc. Their tormentor, at first silhouetted against a pale winter sky, suddenly weaves after them, its form obscured as it twists and turns above the long grass. A boomerang made flesh, freed from the rigid trajectory of its wooden avatar, and able to realise true mastery of the aerial pursuit.

In this hunt, the outcome depends not just on the skill of the hunter but the mistake of the hunted. One false turn, out of sync with the swirling flock, or even a wingbeat or two off the pace, and it's over. The predator inverts, throwing its talons forward to punish the deviant. In such a high-speed chase, impact can mean instant death – if the victim is lucky. Less fortunate prey are stunned but still alive, bound in the agonizing grasp of talons, swung forward so the hooked beak can finish it off with a nip to the neck. Then, it's off to the plucking post.

The flock alights again. Calm resumes across the wetland after the brief but furious incursion. The songbirds continue their harvest of seeds and grubs among the grass and low bushes, mercifully spared by the falcon.

●●●

I love raptors. Though I like all birds, birds of prey have always had a special fascination for me. The power, the elegance of form, the eyesight on a level far eclipsing our own ... it all made for an avian enigma, augmented by how elusive they so often proved.

And then there are the talons. As a boy who grew up on dinosaur books – and someone still enamoured with the ties between dinosaur and bird – I saw in the raptor's talons the perfected descendent of the killing claws of their Cretaceous namesakes. Now, it isn't the middle toe, with the switchblade raised, that does the knife work. In modern raptors it's almost invariably the hallux, at the back of the foot, folding home to complete the clasp, that kills the prey.

Long ago, the raptors carved up predatory duties among themselves. Owls laid claim not to a certain prey but a certain time; with few exceptions they hunt from dusk till dawn, a time when few other birds can find purchase on food with eyes trained for the daylight. Eagles are the powerhouses of the family, the big-game hunters. Vultures are the undertakers, charged with recycling the corpses left behind in the wake of illness, predators and old age. This is no easy task, for carrion is always in hot demand and they must often soar huge distances to find it.

The hawks we know diverged along two broadly different paths some time ago: the *accipters* (think our sparrowhawk) are terrors of the forests, menacing songbirds as they weave between the trees on short, rounded wings; the *buteos* (think buzzard), bulky and barrel chested, soar in the open, typically targeting the rabbits and other small mammals that graze nervously in meadows around the world. Kites and harriers rival the *buteos* in size but are often more buoyant, preferring to take smaller morsels, even insects and earthworms.

And then there are the falcons, the avian spitfires. In their introductory blurb on the *falco* genus, field guides so often focus on the 'tooth', referring to the spike on the upper mandible. This serves as a sidearm to help dispatch prey.

But for me, having first flicked through guides to the birds of Ireland as a child, it's always been the eyes: seemingly pure black, as if the pupil has consumed the rest of the surface to soak up every drop of light it can. In this respect, falcons are almost totally unlike any other birds of prey. And even on a moving bird at a distance, they can sometimes be seen clearly. Most often for me they're encased in the head of the kestrel that haunts the banks of the river near my home, waiting in the wind for rodents to leave their ultraviolet calling cards, the drops of urine that will draw their reckoning to them. The black crown jewels of the kestrel can venture into a colour spectrum beyond that of human sight, and it is this that guides them through the grassy labyrinth.

We have three native falcons in Ireland. The peregrine is the king; at full dive, it's the fastest animal on Earth, tearing down cliff faces and mountainsides with such velocity that it can decapitate its victim on impact. By far the most familiar is the kestrel. It's perhaps our commonest raptor (though the sparrowhawk could also stake a claim). The kestrel thrives in the grassy verges that border our main roads. Here it hovers (the only falcon we have that does so) with consummate patience, waiting for its prey to betray its presence before descending in steps, readjusting coordinates for the final pounce.

Then there's the merlin, the smallest of the three. Rather than relying on patience or a devastating dive, the merlin is a pursuit hunter, winning its meals through agility and perseverance. While the peregrine rains death on its victim from above, the merlin hunts lower to the ground, often forcing its victim skyward. Twisting and turning on frantic wingbeats, it's as if the bird delights in exhausting and outmanoeuvring its prey. Where possible, the merlin will give itself the edge by ambushing its victim on the ground, sullying it with a standing start. Even when flying about in the open, the rapid, flicking flight style of the merlin evokes that of a thrush, allowing it to disguise itself in plain sight – until it is close enough to give chase.

Birds of prey are famously dimorphic; females are larger than males in a reversal of vertebrate norms. In the falcons this is particularly pronounced. The male is a third smaller than the female, leading to the name 'tiercel'. Given this, gender roles play a key part in merlin life. The slate-grey tiercel, smaller and swifter than his mate, uses his speed to poach small passerines in flight. The bulkier female, with more punch to her killer blow, can tackle larger songbirds, up to the size of thrushes. Sometimes the pair will even work together to win a meal: one bird flushes the prey, the other takes it out. Between them, they provide a regular protein supply for young merlins each spring, reared in treetop eyries in mountain ranges across Ireland. At first the male does the bulk of the hunting, but once the chicks have matured enough for the female to vacate the nest, she chips in to fuel their rapid growth.

It is in its springtime demesne that the merlin resumes its rivalry with another inhabitant of our mountainsides: the skylark. Every breeding season, this rambunctious songbird can be heard blasting out a winding stream of notes from high in the air, wings beating frantically to keep it aloft.

Skylarks are among the merlin's favourite prey in Ireland, second only to the meadow pipit. The male skylark's song, as with that of almost all birds, is used to attract a mate and declare territory. But it also plays a vital role in the species' relationship with the merlin. The fittest males can sing mid-air with the most vigour – and typically, it is these males who are spared the killing embrace of the merlin.

Silent males, or poor singers, are not so fortunate. Like the merlin, the skylark is an accomplished aerial acrobat. But only males with a powerful singing voice – a vocal expression of their flying prowess – can hope to outpace the merlin in an airborne dogfight. Less accomplished songsters stand a better chance if they simply drop to the floor and stay out of sight. Because of this, the airborne singing of a strong, healthy skylark is akin to the prancing of a svelte antelope on the savannah. It advertises fitness and virility, as alluring to a prospective mate as it is dissuasive to a hungry merlin. A predator's energies are better spent in pursuit of a slower target. It's just one way the merlin has helped prune the skylark population to peak fitness, and hone its mating rituals over many generations. Concomitantly, faster skylarks have undoubtedly left slower merlins to starve in their wake over the eons, leading to the refinement of the tenacious pursuit predator that torments their descendants today.

Treetop nesting does not come naturally to merlins in Ireland. Traditionally birds of uplands in spring, for generations merlins nested amongst heather, seeing off any avian interlopers with ruthless aggression. As afforestation has ravaged the uplands, they've increasingly taken to nesting in trees, commandeering disused corvid nests for their own ends.

Perversely, merlin chicks born in trees are often more likely to fledge than their counterparts on the ground, perhaps because there are fewer predators to threaten them high in the branches. But this dramatic change in the landscape hasn't been entirely beneficial for our smallest raptor. The razor-sharp, pointed wings of the merlin are designed for pursuit in open terrain; this is not a bird of confined, wooded spaces, where the broad, rounded wings of the sparrowhawk come into their own. The loss of the heather has shrunk the available habitat in which breeding merlins feel most at home.

The merlin is not as cosmopolitan as our other falcons. Kestrels, predators of farmland and road verges, are easy cohabitants with humans. Among the peregrine's favourite prey are pigeons – pigeons that thrive like rats in urban spaces. Because of this, peregrines have followed their ambitious human counterparts from the remote hillsides and clifftops to the cities in search of an easier life. They've taken to hunting amidst high-rises and quarries, and the crannies atop churches and cathedrals make ideal nesting spots.

In general, the merlin hasn't transitioned as well to the world of man. The bulk of its small Irish breeding population remains confined to the shrinking pool of suitable upland habitat each spring. This makes it one of our more difficult birds of prey to find, and much cherished amongst birders.

Like its cousin the peregrine, the merlin was also hit hard by pesticide poisoning, building up through the eco-system to impact the predators at the top. In North America, where the merlin–peregrine dynamic also exists, this even led to a curious shift in merlin behaviour. When the peregrine went into decline, the merlin suddenly found itself the top falcon on the winter wetlands of Washington

State. With no peregrines to challenge them, the merlins started hunting more in the open with a swagger becoming of an apex predator. However, when peregrine numbers rebounded, the merlins resumed the low-to-the-ground hunting more typical of their species. Perhaps this was to avoid the wrath of the peregrine – they both dined on the same prey, and a peregrine is certainly large enough to make a meal of a merlin.

Wetlands are oases for birdlife in winter. It is here that the merlins typically descend to after their upland bounty has run out and the weather starts to turn (though some males lag behind in the mountains to hold on to their cherished breeding territories). This is when the merlin becomes a menace along our coasts, often perching on logs and other flotsam to catch its breath or enjoy a kill after another frantic chase.

It is in the hopes of seeing one of these wintering hunters that I make my way to Dundalk, County Louth, home to one of the largest areas of exposed mudflats in the country. It's exactly the kind of place that wintering merlins frequent.

●●●

The main street is desolate. Pubs, bookies and antique shops are locked up for Sunday. There are no signs of the Saturday night carnage as the road leads onto a bridge crossing the Castletown River. To my left, the vast banks are coated in grass stretching away into the countryside. To the right, the Castletown meanders restlessly towards Dundalk Bay.

The bay is one of Ireland's largest natural harbours. It is this strategic advantage that has drawn envious invaders to Dundalk over the centuries. Ancient settlers were quick to establish themselves in this area, leaving a legacy of passage tombs in their wake. Later, the Normans, upon prosecuting their conquest of Ireland, made a point of settling in Dundalk, at the northern reaches of the Pale, facilitating as it did easy trade with Britain.

This corner of Ireland was also amongst the first to experience the wrath of the New Model Army – although Dundalk was spared the worst of the bloodletting. Hearing of the horrors that beset their compatriots in nearby Drogheda, the people of Dundalk surrendered to Cromwell without a fight. The peace that followed the ravages of the Irish Confederate Wars allowed the port to thrive, and industries like linen and brewing to flourish in the town. The resulting prosperity would manifest in Dundalk's distinctly Victorian character, still discernible today in stately churches, cobbled streets and weathered shopfronts given new leases of life as boutiques and ethnic food outlets.

Crossing the bridge on a chilly February morning, it doesn't take long for the first signs of birdlife to reveal themselves. Black-headed gulls bathe with vigour in the shallows, beating water over their backs with cupped wings. The mud pooled at the riverside serves as a jetty for lapwings, grounded by the stiff breeze. They turn their masked faces towards me in unison, streamlining themselves against the wind, two-pronged crests whipping like a helmet weathervane. Behind them, the detritus of the river – crisp packets, beer bottles, plastic wrappers – gathers amongst flattened reeds. Snipe shelter here in clusters, lending a golden-brown sheen to an otherwise drab, polluted scene. They seem content to conceal themselves amongst man-made squalor, oblivious as to how their colour is its only saving grace.

The riverside, though, is no place for a merlin, and so I start to follow the Castletown towards the sea. On the far bank, gulls of a myriad of whites and greys dot the shoreline. Those that brave the harsh wind swirling in from the coast hang in suspended animation, as if strung from the ceiling of a child's bedroom. That same wind whips the river below them into a moiling swell. I can only imagine how cold it must be. At intervals, a cormorant surfaces, draped in beads dredged up from the depths, tiny pupils fixed in green eyes giving it a startled expression.

The path that traces the riverside overshadows a rocky shoreline, festooned with dank seaweed. Every few minutes, a redshank bursts from the shore with a panicked cry, only to be defeated by the wind and land just a few metres away. More at ease are the ruffs that also feed amongst the rocks. This can be a hard species to see in Ireland; Dundalk is one of the best spots for them. In summer, the males sport one of the most spectacular feathered appendages of any bird: the eponymous ruff, like a lion's mane but more refined, forming a hat atop their head and curling around to complete a beard. This can vary from rufous to black or white, giving a selection of colours for the females to choose from at the communal leks where breeding males establish their credentials.

Sadly, wintering ruffs lose their fair-weather glad rags, attaining the more modest greys and browns typical of visiting waders, scalloped wings a souvenir of recent splendour. Robbed of their headgear, the males can look tragically plain, even potbellied, with their protruding midriff accentuated by the elongated neck and small head and bill. It's as if they've purposefully flocked to a town once pregnant with Victorian vigour, in the hopes that some of this will rub off and restore the ruff that was the height of aristocratic fashion in days gone by. But even without their crowning glory, they can still strike a handsome figure in the morning light, periodically piercing through the clouds to lend them an ochre hue.

A few streets of terraced houses. A Gaelic football field sprinkled with oystercatchers, orange bills nestled beneath black wings. Rounding the bend, the mouth of the Castletown re-emerges before me. On the near side, the muddy bank rises steeply towards a wall. Across the river, skeletal vestiges of ruined wooden structures protrude at odd angles from the water. Each, to my eager mind, would make a perfect perch for a raptor, offering a commanding view of the wetland and the ducks and waders laid out in legions across its surface. But there's no merlin in sight.

Not that Dundalk Bay is wanting for wildlife in their absence. The place is flowing with birds. Beyond the mudflats on the far bank, low reed beds, like a wheat field gone feral, stretch out into the distance. The Mourne Mountains are hazy on the horizon. Closer to, the café-au-lait brown of the mudflats is broken by a vast line of shimmering grey: knots, aligned in their thousands, every single one with their heads buried in their backs, as if in formation. Amidst their ranks one renegade stands out – bright red, a precocious romantic already in full breeding finery. A soldier of spring, surrounded by the grey phalanx of winter.

Fortunately, he's not the only colour to be found on the riverside. Shelducks, with greens and oranges peeling into white, patrol the shoreline. More numerous are the teal, the males with their striking green-and-red helmets, filtering their way through the shallows. And at the heart of the river, a pair of red-breasted mergansers dive and surface in unison, like a submarine ballet. Lounging on the surface, pulsating with the waves, the male's crest is battered around by the incessant wind.

I find so often with birdwatching it can be the stillness that stirs the life around you. It's as if motion is one half of a totality, and your motionlessness forces the creatures in your shadow to move to restore the balance. If you stop to admire the glowing blooms of a gorse bush, the linnets within will erupt in a cacophony of chirps and white-bladed wings. Taking in the view from a seaside path, you'll often send the curlews and godwits below scurrying for safety. If they'd just stood still you'd have been none the wiser to their presence.

It's the same with birds of prey. When looking for raptors, unless they're on territory, I often find your best hope is to let other birds do the hard work. These birds, with sharp eyes honed by instinct to react with revulsion to raptors, will usually be the first to spot the predator – and respond with venom. Buzzards, for instance, often have their presence betrayed by the cohort of irate corvids they draw into their orbit. Crows rarely shy away from challenging raptors – especially when they have numbers on their side.

Smaller passerines can't do this. Usually they flock together, giving them the double advantage of more eyes to spot a predator, and more bodies to make it less likely you end up in the predator's scope. When a raptor is spotted, instead of mounting an offensive, they take off in collective panic; a tornado of feathers intended to confuse their tormentor. This is usually the giveaway that a threat has been spotted. And it's the smaller raptors, the falcons, the ones that take songbirds on the wing, which elicit the most potent response. Birds as big as a buzzard rarely bother with starlings or finches (and could almost never catch them even if they did). Instead, it's the boomerang wings of the falcon, that consummate aerial killer, that strike them with the deepest fear. And so it is this response that I search for across the expanse of the mudflats.

Hope overtakes me whenever I see the redshanks, dunlins and shelducks on the opposite bank burst into flight. Periodically, amidst the probing and sifting of mud by bills long or flat, there's an almighty commotion. Dunlins whirl with white bellies flashing. Shelducks lumber into the air in twos and threes. *This is it*, I keep thinking. *The hunt is on.*

But it's a hollow hunt. There is no raptor to be seen as I scan the riverbank. Perhaps it's a fox skulking amongst the reeds, a mink slithering out of the murk, or just a collective compulsion to seek a less-exposed section of mud on which to shelter from the breeze. Whatever's disturbed the ducks and waders, it's no raptor.

The long path tracing the river finally terminates at Soldier's Point. It's crowned with a haunting sculpture entwining a boat with a sepulchral human figure, as if in joint homage to Dundalk's maritime tradition and also the past horrors visited on the people of this area. It recalls a time when not just airborne vagabonds made their way to Dundalk. Being a prominent port, during the Famine the town served as an exit point for thousands of desperate emigrants, searching for salvation overseas.

Below, the briars spread out past the last houses, a writhing mass of botanical carnage, crudely held back by slanting fences. I can make out no birds, much less raptors, amid the morass. The beating wind, with no features natural or man-made to impede it, makes it difficult for birds to make any headway. Most cling to the ground, hidden amongst the thorns. Beyond the briars, the mouth of the river is whipped into a swell. Winter still holds the bay in a merciless embrace, like talons, borne in of an eastern breeze, grasping at the exposed belly that is where Dundalk meets the sea.

But the battle of the seasons is a precarious one. By late morning, as I approach the spot where my sojourn began, the expanse of the Castletown River is bathed in sunlight. The breeze eases. If only for a moment, it feels like winter is in retreat, and has surrendered the town around me to the spring. In its wake, winter soldiers are left stranded on the muddy banks of the river: ruffs, in pairs, patrol the shallows, scalloped feathers unassuming, not yet succumbing to the aristocratic beauty they will soon assume. More stately are the godwits, long bills buried beneath the water's surface, that sewing machine motion as they pry a steadfast worm from its burrow. And, among them, something special.

Amidst the redshanks dotted across the riverbank, I notice one, paler and thinner than the others, pirouetting in the water, like a dog chasing its tail. A darker stripe through the eye, and a bicoloured bill narrowing to a droop (think a drop of blood pooling at the end of a syringe) clinches the ID: a spotted redshank, a rare winter visitor, and another bird with a penchant for Dundalk and its surrounds. It's a good find – some would say better than a merlin. Spinning about in the water on legs that seem almost too thin for its body, the bird pitches forwards mid-circuit, as if its head is suddenly too heavy to hold up. From the footpath I watch this ensemble of waders, the rare mingling with the common, none of them nervous about my presence. With birdwatching, you sometimes don't always get what you want. But often, you get so much more.

My quarry has eluded me. But the search must go on. High-concept wildlife documentaries require months or years of toil, with untold near misses. Finding my merlin won't be so arduous. On a wetland not so far flung, or a mountainside bog in spring, it's waiting on its plucking post.

The sun creeping higher over Dundalk starts to warm my cheeks. Spring is on the march. Soon the ruffs and the godwits and the spotted redshanks will all be gone, an army of winter lodgers departing for the far north. But in their wake will come other visitors to fill the void.

A feast of spring and summer birding awaits.

GOOSANDER

Glendalough

It begins on the path. The sunlight of a March morning cuts through the lobed leaves of the oak canopy. Steam flows from every breath; scarves wrapped tight against the cold. A trickle of muddy water flanks the path on one side, overhung by mossy boulders. On the other, the land angles down towards the valley floor, forested all the way.

Before long, my friend Mark and I come to an aisle of skeletal birch and ash shrubs, stripped of leaves by a winter just ended. Families of long-tailed tits pirouette about the twigs above us, hoovering up any invertebrates stirred to life by the inklings of spring. Fresh buds provide the only greenery. They also make a ripe harvest for bullfinches, flitting through the shrubbery.

We soon emerge at the valley floor. At its heart lies the ancient church of St. Saviour, roofless from centuries of neglect.

The holy men who sought God in Glendalough could scarcely have picked a better spot for their church. Even a sceptic can admit that it commands a captivating view of creation. The brook that tinkles beside the church is hemmed in by hills. They are crested with conifers on one side and threadbare deciduous trees on the other. It's as if each clan has staked its claim to either bank, with occasional copses breaking the trend, the vanguard of some horticultural crusade across the valley, forays onto enemy soil.

The conifers are crawling with songbirds. Siskin, blue tit and chaffinch all poke their heads out from between the needles. Blackbirds and song thrush are in full verse. Every half hour or so, there's the squawk of a pheasant. Further afield, the drumming of great spotted woodpeckers adds percussion to the ensemble. But the great tit champions them all with its relentless two-toned cry. Great tits are notorious bullies at bird feeders, and their competitive personalities also manifest in song. Long after the other birds have desisted, the gnawing *teacher, teacher* call still rings out across the valley.

So much is patience with birdwatching. I think of sitting in hides overlooking reed beds or staking out valleys for raptors that fail to manifest. But sometimes nature is generous. A morning such as this was proof.

The stream bisecting the valley flows right past St. Saviour's Church, which is itself ringed by a mossy ridge. No sooner had we poked our heads over this, to gaze at the amber stream below, and there they were. Four goosanders in two handsome pairs, as if taken straight from the pages of a guidebook; the females with copper heads and silver backs, the males with their stunning white chest, black saddle and green head, darker still in the shadow of the trees. For both sexes, a blood red bill, drooping at the tip, completes the package.

It is so quick I only have time to note their fine details before the flotilla, hurried but not panicked into flight, makes its way downstream, heads turned at 45-degree angles to keep us in view. The tangled undergrowth soon obscures them, and they vanish around a bend in the distance.

•••

Goosanders are one of a brace of breeding ducks we have known as the sawbills (a third, the smew, is a scarce winter visitor). It is the largest of this family of ducks, which derive their name from the notched, fish-eating accoutrement they carry. Not for the sawbills is the clumsy, spoon-shaped beak of the dabbling ducks, the mallards that throng on urban waterways begging for bread from passers-by or the flocks that colour our wetlands each winter. Most of these birds, despite spending so much of their time on the water, can scarcely upend to crane for a seed beyond the reach of their outstretched neck.

Not so the sawbills. Never content to languish at the surface, they get their food by diving. And far from subsisting on debris floating on the water's surface, or grazing on waterside meadows like avian ungulates, they've embraced a predatory lifestyle, pursuing fish and invertebrates with singular agility.

As with most birds that have taken to the water, their webbed feet are placed far back on the body for maximum propulsion underwater. (This, though, leaves them at a disadvantage on land, where they can only amble awkwardly.) And like most avian fishermen, they track down their prey by sight. In the case of the goosander, they frequently dip their heads beneath the water, scoping out the submerged surrounds for a meal. Once a fish has been spotted (amphibians and insects are also taken) the chase begins. If successful, the goosander usually surfaces with prey in its beak. Tenderly tossing it around in its saw bill, the meal is then swallowed headfirst, ensuring no spiny fins get caught and easing its passage down the bird's throat.

Fishing is when the saw bill comes in handy. Running up and down its length are tiny serrations, hooking backwards to secure tight purchase on slimy prey. In this way, the sawbills harken back to some of the most primitive birds, flightless behemoths who snapped up fish with toothed beaks while their dinosaur cousins still dominated on land. The goosander, though, is a bird of flight. Like all modern birds it has abandoned teeth entirely in order to shed the weight needed to take wing. The serrations, though, are about as close as any modern bird comes.

The bill also has use during courtship. In the mating season, displaying males elongate their necks and bills skywards to their fullest extent, cutting circles in the water as they bid to woo passing females.

The goosander shares its saw bill with its close cousin, the red-breasted merganser. At first glance, they appear similar. But there are important differences. Mergansers, for one, are primarily birds of our coasts, gathering in sheltered harbours by winter where they can fish in relative safety from the tumult of the open sea. Though attractive birds, their plumage is not clear cut; the colours merge and dilute, as if the bird has thrown on its cosmetics all in a hurry, only to have them blurred and sullied by the water.

The goosander is a bird of wild lakes and rivers, only haunting the coasts in winter. And its sublime plumage (sans the windswept crest of the merganser) always retains its clear demarcations, especially in the male: that luscious green head atop a white nick and chest, flanked by darker wing markings.

Preferring, as it does, forested habitats within touching distance of fresh water, the goosander has adopted a breeding strategy you'd think anathema for a duck, especially one so large (significantly bigger than most you'll find at your local pond). It routinely nests in tree holes, a habit normally reserved for the much smaller songbirds with which it shares its woodland home. It's as if the peculiarities of passerine-hood have rubbed off on the goosander, and so it endeavours to stake a claim to the most prized of nesting real estate the forest has to offer.

Selecting a suitable nest site is the task of the female goosander. Her standards are exacting – and they have to be. Finding a tree hole large enough to house a family of goosanders is challenging enough. But the need to overshadow running water restricts the goosander's nesting choices even further. It is onto this water (or, at the very least, a soft surface near the water) that young goosanders – still flightless – must crash when they leave the nest for the first time, or else risk a fatal fall straight onto solid ground.

Most tree holes don't meet the criteria: big enough to house the female and her brood at a squeeze, while being close enough to a stream or lakeside to allow a safe landing for the chicks. It's not unheard of for hole-ridden trees to play host to several goosander families. Once she's found a hole that satisfies her, the female fashions the bottom into a bowl, lining it with soft down plucked from her own breast. However, the chicks don't get to enjoy this cosy bedding for long. Within forty-eight hours of hatching their mother's call tempts them from the nest, out onto the water below.

In their generosity, conservationists have erected nest boxes in Glendalough that the birds have readily taken to. In their absence, and if there's a dearth of tree holes, goosanders are forced to compromise, making their homes under mossy boulders or even in the gutted ruins of homesteads. This means a walk over land for the female and her chicks to reach the lake or stream. Here, the youngsters are fed on aquatic invertebrates until they're ready for the fish that will sustain them for the rest of their lives.

●●●

Excitement over, the monotony of birdwatching returns. We know the goosanders are nesting nearby, and will not stay away for long. So we decide to stake out this spot, waiting for their nervousness to abate before they make the brief flight back upstream. And so we settle into the streamside, peppered with deer dung, to await their return.

In my yearning for a second look, my mind begins to get the better of me. Fleets of bubbles float by, sometimes forming large clumps of white froth, and I'm all too keen to mistake this for the white chest of the male goosander.

Frustrated, I lie back to take in the sights of the valley around me. Among the conifers, houses stud the slope rising above the stream. Down river, the valley floor gives way to pasture. Here, sheep roam freely. Lambs, with long, curving tails, frolic. In the field on the far bank, a brace of hinds bolt for cover, white rumps taking up the rear. The deer know the best way through this valley, and it is so often their paths that we follow through the long grass, dusted with ice like the leaves of the trees shadowing the stream. By now, the rising sun has come to collect its toll. As the branches begin to weep, large drops splatter on my shoulders.

Beside us, the river is the colour of lager. It's barely a metre deep, and on its bed smooth stones are sprinkled with the minerals that drew generations of miners to Glendalough. Panning would bring us little fortune here though, for anything that could be strained from this stream would be too little and too poor to be worth the effort.

I can see no signs of life in the water as it leisurely makes its way to the lake. I wonder how piscivores like the goosander draw enough sustenance from Glendalough, especially given that the waters of the upper lake (the largest in the valley) are notoriously acidic. But being predators, goosanders are often seen as a benchmark of the health of the rivers and lakes they call home. Their presence in Glendalough is a measure of the fecundity of its waters. In any case, acidity can bestow a clarity to the water. This can help the goosanders zero in on what fish there are here.

In an age when many birds seem to be beating a retreat in the wake of the devastation left by man, it's exciting that (for now) the goosander is on the march. Not thirty years ago, breeding pairs were almost unheard of in Ireland. At the time, this was no surprise. The ducks Irish people are most familiar with are birds of temperate wetlands. Their docile dabbling nature has eased their transition into an increasingly human world.

But the goosander is not most ducks. By nature, it's a creature of the wild boreal forests, that vast coniferous belt that hangs like a curtain just below the icy grip of the Arctic. It's a harsh realm, shared with wolves and bears. Wintering goosanders rarely made it as far south as Ireland, So while wigeon, teal and other ducks could (and still can) be found in flocks of hundreds all around our coasts each winter, for many years the only glimpse you'd get of a goosander in Ireland (if you were lucky) was of a green- or copper-headed speck patrolling an estuary.

That all changed in 1994 when goosanders were recorded breeding in County Wicklow for the very first time. The species had previously tried to establish an outpost in Donegal, but while this attempt to colonise

Ireland eventually petered out, the Wicklow population has endured.

In so doing, goosanders have added Ireland to the expanding list of countries in which they have made a permanent home, having colonised vast swathes of Britain in the previous decades and even claimed a toehold in the Alps. Although they've bred in Ireland every year since 1994, the population here remains small and centred around its stronghold in the Wicklow Mountains.

Here, where the valleys vacated by long-gone glaciers have been occupied by fresh mountain lakes, the species has found its Shangri-la. And they're not the first to find peace and prosperity in this valley. The most famous to do so was St. Kevin, who found in Glendalough the perfect place to establish his monastery back in the sixth century. St. Kevin was renowned as a great lover of nature, as one of the most famous legends of his life in Glendalough – documented in *The Church and Kindness to Animals* – attests:

> And while he was lifting up his hand to heaven through the window, as he used to do, a blackbird by chance alighted on it, and treating it as a nest, laid an egg there. And the Saint showed such compassion towards it, out of his patient and loving heart, that he neither closed his hand nor withdrew it, but indefatigably held it out and adapted it for the purpose until the young one was fully hatched.

But Kevin's avian associations stretch even further into legend. Perhaps the most striking recalls how he first laid claim to Glendalough. At that time, the O'Tooles were among the most powerful of the Gaelic families in the region. Their king, grief-stricken over the ill health of his aging pet goose, reached out to Kevin to help save the bird. Kevin agreed – but only if he could have all the land that the goose flew over. Sure enough, with a touch from Kevin the goose regained a youthful vigour. It took off in a circuit around the valley that we now know as Glendalough.

It was here that Kevin sought the solitude in which he could immerse himself in God's living work, eschewing the company of people for that of the birds and beasts that thrived in the valley. Back then, the goosander was almost certainly not among them, though it's ironic that the vacuum left by one departing hermit has centuries later been filled by an avian recluse that has found sanctuary in Glendalough.

In a crueller irony, it was the teachings of the solitude-loving St. Kevin that would see the solitude of Glendalough shattered. Kevin was one of Ireland's most accomplished and well-travelled Christian scholars (even journeying to Rome and back). As recorded in *Bethada Náem nÉrenn*:

> Great is the pilgrimage of Coemgen (as Kevin was
>   then known),
> If men should perform it aright;
> To go seven times to his fair is the same
> As to go once to Rome.

To claim that seven visits to this valley in the Wicklow Mountains was the spiritual equal to a pilgrimage to the centre of Western Christendom was a bold idea for the time. But it soon took root. And so St. Kevin's teachings spawned a monastic tradition that turned Glendalough into one of the centres of Christian teaching in Ireland in the centuries after his death. A monastery flourished here, complete with its own cathedral and round tower to safeguard monks and their treasures from the Vikings that raided their way up and down the east coast.

It wasn't just the divine that enticed settlers to Glendalough, but also the prosaic. The tectonic churning that raised the Wicklow Mountains forged at their heart seams of lead, silver and other ores that drew a mining community to the valley. By the middle of the 1800s they'd become well established, tunnelling deep into the mountain slopes in pursuit of wealth. At the height of the mining boom over two thousand people lived here. The scale of their operations soon outmatched the mules and other draught animals used to haul chunks of ore to processing, and so a railway had to be introduced to take up the load.

Hunger for wealth drove further development along the valley. New seams were cut open and worked to their roots. The miners' labour beneath the mountains took them so far from the comforts of the Wicklow coast that one mine was even named Van Diemen's Land in tribute to the island (present day Tasmania) on the other side of the globe, where many Irish convicts of the day were shipped, and from where very few returned. Buildings sprung up in the miners' village on the valley floor, including a water-powered crusher to pulverise the ore peeled from the mountains. This was mainly operated by the women of the village as their husbands and sons toiled by torchlight underground.

Outside, centuries of development had wrought a heavy price on the once pristine wilds of Glendalough. Very little of the ancient forest that once carpeted the valley remains today, with much of the greenery to be found now dating from just the nineteenth century or later.

By the late 1800s the mining community had begun to suffer. More and more of its members took their expertise overseas, where they used it to develop the extraction industries that would fuel manufacturing booms in Britain and the United States. Increased demand for lead during the First World War would see a temporary flowering of mining fortunes, but once the Treaty of Versailles had been signed the mines of Glendalough sunk into decline again. By the late 1950s they were abandoned altogether.

Both the monks and the miners, the pious and the enterprising, left their mark on Glendalough. The round tower, now restored, still stands proud, keeping company with a smattering of other monastic buildings. More solitary, the church of St. Saviour, now haunted by nearby nesting goosanders, lies in ruins, though the Romanesque curves of its arches and blotches of lichen crawling across its stonework still lend it colour and grace.

The miners' legacy is somewhat less striking. You can still find the rusting remains of the crusher, lying otherwise much as it was when working. Among the other remnants they left behind are piles of excavated stone dumped on the valley floor. During childhood visits with my family, I can remember climbing among them, the miner in me looking for the crystal that would make my fortune. And there were indeed crystals to be found on the slag heaps, encrusted onto stone like icing on a cake. But the generations that came before had left no great mineral treasure in Glendalough. Far from twinkling with every caress of the sun, the crystals I unearthed were murky, like frosted glass; hardly the stuff of wedding rings.

Today, the most striking living legacies of human habitation in Glendalough are the feral goats that still patrol the valley. These are not native, but were introduced to provide meat, milk and labour to bygone settlers before escaping (or simply outlasting) their masters, who would desert the valley. Now, they can be seen grazing out in the rushes on the valley floor, or picking their way with delicate care up the scree-strewn slopes of the mountainsides. Crowned with great ridged horns and curtained by flowing coats of grey and black hair, they remain as a visceral reminder of the shifting fortunes of this valley.

Even in boyhood, when its history had not made such an impact on me, Glendalough left a strong impression. This was especially true of the upper lake, its shoreline of flattened, silvery stone blurring into a vast dark abyss. It was like a black hole at the heart of the valley towards which trees marched and mountains descended to their doom. Chinos rolled up above my knees, I'd splash through the shallows, never fearing I'd snag my foot on a sharp rock, for the stones that made up the lake floor had long since surrendered their hooks and corners to the perpetual caress of gentle waves.

Looking back now, I can understand why pious folk found peace on its shores. Rarely stirring to a swell, the lake exudes tranquillity, and an ethereal quality. I imagined that peace would come undone at any moment. My boyhood self hoped this would come in the form of a monster surging up from the depths, for in my head I compared the upper lake to Loch Ness, and used it as the setting for my own fruitless monster hunts. Though no unknown beasts ever greeted me at their end, childhood vignettes in Glendalough helped awaken my yearning for nature. And hikes up its slopes exposed me to the sheer beauty buried in Wicklow's mountainous heart.

The waters of the lake might be too shallow (and devoid of prey) to sustain a hidden monster. But the goosanders find all the food they need in the two lakes (lower and upper) that give Glendalough its name (*Gleann dá Locha*, the glen of the two lakes) and the streams that feed into them. Clear, shallow waters suit them down to the ground. Seeing them here amid the drumming of the great spotted woodpecker (another recent colonist) adds a whole new dimension to Glendalough for me. It feels like a potent commitment by the natural world to restock this space with wild denizens, among them a new cast of characters to augment the fauna of the Wicklow Mountains.

Otters and minks might provide some competition, but not enough to threaten the goosanders. The biggest danger they face comes in the form of another mustelid (weasel) and, ironically, another species that every effort is being made to preserve: the pine marten. Wicklow is one of the strongholds of the pine marten resurgence in Ireland. And while this arboreal sharpshooter is the ideal tonic to the feral population of grey squirrels now rampant throughout the county, it certainly won't refuse the succulent eggs and chicks of goosanders. Nesting in trees puts these ducks at risk of pine marten predation. That's why many of the trees bearing goosander nest boxes are enclosed with sheaths of metal on their trunks; the marten's claws can get no purchase on the metal, and their designs on the goosander's brood can be thwarted.

●●●

As can happen, the end goal can be found back where you started. Having staked out the riverside for over an hour, we make our way back to the car, content with the fleeting view of fleeing goosanders.

On our way, we approach a bridge fording the same river. That's when we see her. Right on the riverbank, perched on a rock, almost completely obscured by the overgrown grass, is the female. As with almost all ducks, her livery pales in comparison to the male. But in the shaft of sunlight breaking through the canopy, she's still stunning: her head a rich copper, her back silver cut through by the outline of her feathers. Slowly, like a ballerina in motion, she extends her neck, perhaps forcing a stubborn fish down her throat.

We're much closer than before. And yet she shows no signs of panic, even though she can surely see us towering on the bank above her. It's only then we notice the male, approaching her on the languid current. She slides into the water beside him, and together they make their way downstream. The light on him is less forgiving; he clings to the shadows of the opposite bank, frustrating my urge to get a decent photo of his stunning green head. But the pleasure of seeing them so close – and so unhurried – is compensation enough.

As the procession slips downstream, a second female joins the couple; the second male is nowhere to be seen. Breaking into a light jog, we follow them to the bridge, watching them pass under us. Once again, their heads are angled to keep us in view, but there is no urgency in their cruising. They're more than happy to let the stream dictate the tempo of their journey: free birds, floating.

The amber water beneath them glistens and sparkles, as if the riverbed were studded with gold. It's like the miners of old have foolishly left a fortune behind. And as the goosanders float over it, they pass under branch after branch, until finally they melt away into the overhanging undergrowth.

GREY PARTRIDGE

Lough Boora

The setting is rural Ireland at its most pristine. Offaly is among the flattest of Ireland's counties, with only a distant plateau adding any bulk on the horizon. Closer to, the fields are lightly dusted with frost, the morning dew crystalised by the March chill.

In the early morning the rooks are in full voice. From the unkempt balls of twigs in which they nest high in denuded trees, they make a raucous chorus. It's as if each bird can't help but want to out-call its neighbour, and soon the canopy is awash with cawing. Atop a scots pine a lonely mistle thrush watches on in silence, positioned to sing but hesitant to do so, knowing its solo will be drowned out by the relentless chatter of the rookery.

Closer to the ground, more modest songbirds, which don't feel the need to proclaim dominance by assuming a lofty position, make easier purchase on the morning soundscape with their calls. Male blackbirds are on territory, crooning in the low branches of the undergrowth. They share the stage with cock robins, orange feathers bristling with the effort of expelling their rich stream of song. Agitated, they flick from branch to branch, eager to see off any interlopers that might stake a claim to the best perch. Enshrined in menacing thorns, one of their nests sits in a stunted bush by the side of the road. The still-radiant green of the moss woven into the structure is about the only colour to be found amid the tangle of dark twigs and briars. It's like an outpost of spring, a flag declaring to all about the farmland that after a long, cold winter, more fecund days are at hand.

Beyond, the fields spread out across the landscape. In the one closest to me four horses with heavy woollen boots graze, the sun right overhead casting long, four-legged shadows across the grass. They share the fields with a panoply of farmland birds. Hopping along the ground, the mistle thrushes and fieldfares, silver heads glistening in the morning light, frustrate my urge to pick out a distant partridge among the jackdaws, starlings and woodpigeons. Time and again I find myself squeezing a partridge into a thrush, only for the hopping motion to shatter the delusion. They share the upright stance I expect of a partridge, and the mistle thrush even has the same pot belly. But while partridges are primarily grazers, akin to avian guinea pigs, the thrushes busy themselves rooting out worms in the wet earth. They only concede to herbivorous temptation when it's sweet-wrapped in the form of fruit.

On and on the path meanders through the fields, past a barn bursting with cattle and dung heaps sprinkled with ice. Sheep graze, docile, on one side. On the other, a limousin bull, horns blackened at the tips, glares at me as I walk past. He marches forth with purpose, placing himself between me and the cows and calves feeding behind him. For a moment, I wish there were more than a few flimsy strands of barbed wire separating us.

As the sun rises higher, the frost goes into full retreat. The barbed wire is hung with golden droplets, like bunting festooned about the farmland in celebration of spring. In its wake, the melting frost leaves its residue across the grassy fields, and they start to sparkle. They make a perfect course for hares, bounding across the fields in twos and threes every time I draw near. At times, they rock back on their hind legs to scan the surroundings. This is when their size impresses; they're close to twice the size of the rabbits I'd mistaken them to be at a distance.

As it is for the partridges, Lough Boora and its surrounding parkland is a sanctuary for the Irish hare – the only member of its clan native to Ireland. This is one of the few places where they seem to outnumber rabbits, their invasive cousins from the continent. Rabbits are a relic from the days of the Norman adventurers, following them on their conquests across this island. But the hare has been here since at least the end of the last Ice Age, long before the first people.

Unlike rabbits, hares have a penchant for bog land, but can also thrive on farms when there are plentiful hedgerows for them to escape to. And in the now carefully managed environment at Lough Boora, conditions for them (as for the partridge) are perfect. The sheer mass of the hare doesn't lend itself to a subterranean retreat, and so they are forced to shelter out in the open. That leaves them exposed to hunters, human or other. But at Lough Boora, the presence of predators is strictly curbed to allow the partridge to flourish undisturbed. It is this benign human interference that helps other herbivores thrive here too, an Eden where prey sneer at predators from behind the shield of man.

As I venture farther and farther along the trail, the trees vanish, and with them the long-gone caws of the rookery. Instead, the bird calls here are a blend of farm and wetland. The croak of a pheasant mingles with the pews of lapwings, and the honking of distant geese. It feels like Lough Boora cannot decide what kind of aviary it most desires to assemble, and so keeps a wide menagerie in an attempt to please all comers.

[43]

Buried within the mosaic of fields is a designated space solely for nourishing the partridge. Knowing how they thrived in pre-modern farmland, it's not hard to see why. Crossing the threshold, you feel like you've set foot on a Midlands farm as it might have been long ago. The grass is long and golden brown, unchecked by ruminant or machine. The fields here are loosely demarcated, their foliage patchier; meadows, caught somewhere between the wild and tame. Blotchy legumes lend green to the scene. In spots, vestiges of the bog still manage to creep through, the sun-cooked peat crumbling like chocolate cake. Its virility pours into the spring shoots that crest across its surface, in between the patchwork of crops. Combined, they make plentiful cover for the partridge to hide in.

No surprise, then, that they're not the first birds that catch my eyes. Lapwings, another species that thrive in the no-man's land set aside for the partridge, fill the air with synthesised bleeps. On thick, clubbed wings that flick from dark to white, they wheel high and low over the fields, chasing others into the air, enticing them to join in the fun of it all. On the ground they strut about with rear ends held high, a stance more moth than bird. Sometimes, as I follow the trail that encloses the fields, I mistake the tapering tail of a lapwing for the extended neck of a partridge, craning to keep me in view. Overhead, skylarks make a constant murmur, wings beating ceaselessly to hold them aloft. Every now and then, amidst the gargle of notes, they happen upon a phrase they like and repeat it two or three times; an improvising musician hoping to spin a hit song from hours of fruitless exertion.

If the lapwing and skylark are aerial masters, yielding their finest performances on the wing, then the partridge is the terrestrial specialist, preferring to crawl amongst the fields than cast shadows on them from above. Flightless birds are a rarity in the northern hemisphere. In Ireland, we lost our last in 1844, the year when the world's last great auk (a flightless cousin of the razorbill and puffin) succumbed to the rapacious hunting of scientific collectors.

The great auk was the northern hemisphere's answer to the penguins. Most terrestrial flightless birds (of which the dodo is the most famous) evolve on remote islands, un-ravaged by mammalian predators. In such isolated Edens, it's surprising the predictability with which so many birds surrender the hard-won inheritance that is powered flight, in favour of a more leisurely life confined to the ground. The far-flung isles of the Pacific and Indian Oceans were once well stocked with flightless feathered denizens, which included among their number some of the largest birds that ever lived.

Ireland has never quite had the dearth of scurrying, egg-thieving menaces to make true flightlessness feasible, though the closest we've come in living memory to a flightless land bird would almost certainly be the grey partridge. While their close cousins, the grouse, are typically birds of desolate mountain slopes, partridges are most at home in open fields. They are birds of grassland, of prairies, the rabbits of the bird world. Hunched over, they scuttle about the grass in family groups (coveys) preferring to scurry to safety in denser undergrowth whenever danger arises. Flight, that ancestral safety mechanism, is retained only as a final contingency, when the threat is too sudden or too fast to run away from. Then, the partridge take off on whirring wings over the fields. The partridge is sedentary. It has no need to cross oceans for the winter, so the only time it needs to divorce itself from the ground at all is when a predator cannot be hidden from or outrun.

The covey is at the centre of partridge life. Taking to open spaces leaves you more exposed to attack from the air or ground. So, the rules that obligate herding in deer and sheep dictate the same behaviour for the partridge. Plenty of eyes make short work of spotting incoming predators. But this strategy far from guarantees survival for the chicks, many of whom succumb to the usual malaises such as hunger and cold.

To help compensate for this, the mother partridge produces the largest clutch of any Irish bird: twenty-nine eggs is the record, a truly astounding reproductive feat. In a typical covey, the female will be joined by her mate, hatchlings and any of last year's brood that have outlived their first winter. They may also generously open up their group to unrelated adults that have failed to breed, offering them the faint comfort of (greater) safety in numbers. Or perhaps there is just some peace to be had in silent company, foraging in the fields together. Now, in spring, the coveys start to fragment. Maturing partridges begin to coalesce into pairs; the males fan their tales, spread their wings and flash the dark horseshoe across their bellies in a bid to woo a mate. Now they are ready to form their own covey and splinter off from their natal flock.

The partridge chicks, like their counterparts among the mammals that graze the open planes, are precocial. They can walk and follow their mother around within an hour of hatching – and they need to. Not for them is the snug nest of a songbird, tucked away in a thicket, a schiltron of thorns to thwart the efforts of predators. Nesting on the ground, partridge chicks are exposed to all the threats that terrestrial living brings. They have to be mobile at once, or will surely get picked off.

●●●

While the hollowing out of Ireland's once vast, primeval forests to make space for farming might have been devastating for woodland birds, for the grey partridge it was a boon. And in a country that clung to traditional methods of farming for so long, the partridge had, in Ireland, a relatively safe haven. The gentle rhythms of the farm synchronised seamlessly with the partridge's lifestyle, affording ample time for the bird to rear its chicks before the crops or hay were gathered. Even hunting could not dent the partridge's numbers enough to pose any real threat.

But all that was to change with the onset of mechanisation, and more intensive farming, from the 1960s onwards. The attack, as it unfolded, was multi-pronged. Pesticides proved devastatingly effective at ridding fields of insects – and with the insects went the glut of spring protein the young partridges fed on. Combine harvesters wrought a deadly toll on hedgerows, those corridors of shelter the partridge needed to nest in and take cover from predators. When profit took precedence over sustenance, fields were worked for tillage at a rate out of sync with partridge nesting. This saw untold eggs and hatchlings destroyed each season.

The increased potency of herbicides helped give rise to monoculture grasslands. In such spaces there was room for only one plant: that which benefitted the farmer. Weeds and other nuisance plants went into an unprecedented retreat, shrinking the partridge's food source even more.

Lose a plant and you lose not only its seeds and shoots, but also the cavalcade of invertebrates that feed on it. It is these creatures that baby partridges, like many farmland birds, need to build bones and sprout feathers.

All of this gradually rendered the vast swathes of farmland coating the Irish countryside hostile to the partridge. In verdant fields where the bird should have been flourishing, there were no longer any partridge to be found. A creature that was once as much a staple of rural Ireland as the pheasant is today was obliterated. Now, it's one of our rarest breeding birds.

The story is the same across much of Europe, where the grey partridge is one of the most rapidly declining species. In Ireland, it clings on only in a few spots like this small haven in the Midlands, fully protected by law despite being a gamebird much prized on the dinner plate. (The meat is darker and more flavoursome than that of the red-legged partridge, its close cousin and a bird sometimes reared here for shooting.)

The situation was so critical that, at the turn of the millennium, there were feared to be fewer than thirty wild grey partridges left in the whole country. In a desperate attempt to preserve the species here, the Boora bog was leased from Bord na Móna (Ireland's largest peat harvester) and set aside with the specific aim of becoming a partridge nursery. Polish birds were brought in to boost the breeding stock. Being sedentary, partridges rarely stray far from their home ranges, and certainly don't partake in the kind of mammoth migrations typical of more seasonal Irish birds. This left the Irish population in desperate need of assistance, as their continental cousins could not be counted on to repopulate Ireland should the last Irish partridge succumb to a tractor's wheel or fox's jaws.

Now, thanks to careful management, there are a few hundred birds to be found at Lough Boora. It's a heart-warming testament to man's desire to save creatures great and small. While reintroductions of kites and eagles might elicit strong passion amongst birders (and ire among disgruntled farmers) the preservation of the humble partridge is, to me, no less noble a cause. It strikes at the unsentimental heart of conservation: are the more spectacular species more deserving of conservation efforts – and largesse? Everyone knows of the plight of the giant panda. But the equally alarming decline of the giant salamander, a slimy half-way house between lizard and frog, gets altogether less publicity, and elicits fewer heart-felt donations from the wallets of donors.

The happier medium preferred by some is to concentrate on no one species in particular, but instead to save their habitat and the whole host of creatures that call it home. By design or not, this is what has happened in Offaly.

The preservation of the hinterland around Lough Boora has been enabled by the controversial halting of another cherished tradition of the Midlands: turf cutting. The Boora parkland had been a rich source of turf for over half a century. Harvesting turf has been a part of rural Irish life for hundreds of years. Nowhere was this truer than here in the Midlands, possessed of vast turf fields and cut adrift from alternative fuel sources elsewhere.

With the forests of Ireland in retreat, and coal relatively scarce, farmers and villagers of old needed another incendiary instrument with which to warm their homes. Turf was it. Cut peat, the compacted remnants of long-dead plants, once left to dry, formed solid bricks that easily took a flame. The resulting fire would be sublimely hot and, although relatively smokeless, still emit a rich and distinctive scent.

To me, there is no smell which elicits a stronger bridge to bygone Ireland. Closing your eyes, you could just as easily be in a kitchen scene a hundred years gone. It always reminds me of summer visits to a grand aunt and uncle in rural County Carlow. As a child, I'd be enamoured with poking for clues of the past amidst the sods of turf stacked in the corrugated shed: chips of wood jutting out from the surface; frail, tanned roots like a wispy beard strung from a corner, all of them vestiges from a time long passed. Over the years, the bogs of Ireland have also yielded far more substantial relics from yesteryear: the mummified remains of long-dead farmers, or the vast antlers of the giant Irish elk.

As it was for the partridge, mechanisation was also the nemesis of the Irish bog. For generations, turf cutters could do no more damage than the sweat of their own labour could manage. Cutting turf was a tiresome process, performed in stages, often with the entire family taking part. After the surface vegetation was cleared, the turf spade, or *sléan* (with a metal fin on the blade to guide the soft peat into the correct shape) would be put to use. An experienced cutter went with the grain of the bog, a barber learned in how to give the best shave. The trick was to cut inwards rather than down, as if the peat had to be caressed to yield its best harvest. The cut slabs of peat would be laid out in lines and stacked up into rows of little pyramids, left to harden in the wind and sun. Each sod had to be turned ('saved') and stood upright ('footed') to ensure its sides got enough exposure to the elements. Then they would be brought back to the farm or village.

This time-honoured method would fall away once wheeled turf-cutting machines came to market. These juggernauts could strip-mine entire swathes of the bog with ease. This was as much to feed the growing industrial market as to heat Irish homes. But contentious voices began to make themselves heard. Among the most prominent was the renowned British botanist David Bellamy. He regarded Ireland's blanket bogs as ecological oases in need of urgent protection.

Not without cause. As well as a source of warmth and revenue for rural communities, the bogs of Ireland are home to a unique ecosystem. Nowhere is this more potently expressed than in the plants indigenous to the bogs. Foremost among these are the carnivorous plants supplementing the sustenance they draw from sun and soil with live prey. They include the sun dew, a head of delicate tendrils each topped with a tempting droplet; at once sweet enough to entice insects while also sticky enough to entrap them. Once the sundew has sufficient grip on its prey, it folds over to engulf it, beginning the digestion process.

More insidious still is the butterwort, which emerges from its cold-weather stasis in an underground bud as an enchanting blue flower atop a star of green leaves. These leaves harbour the strongest natural adhesives to be found in any plant, their curved sides making escape even more difficult for panicked insects scrambling for freedom. The bladderwort, with multiple yellow flowers springing from its shoot, springs from the pools of water that gather in the depressions of the bog. But beneath the surface, it sheds this innocent pretence. The bladders from which it takes its name are small pouches that the anchorless plant spreads out under the water. Each is a trap waiting to snare invertebrate denizens of the pool. It is these snares that make the bladderwort the fastest herbaceous killer in the world.

With such oddities at risk, it's no surprise the conservationists' views have found purchase among policy makers. Now, turf cutting (even of the relatively benign kind carried out in days long gone) is strictly regulated. By 2030, it'll be finished for good.

It's easier to change laws than people. Old traditions die hard. Since the onset of bans on cutting across many of Ireland's blanket bogs, recalcitrant cutters have run afoul of the law. The winding down of turf-cutting operations has come at the loss of crucial jobs for hard-hit Midlands communities. Conservationists remain obstinate that the fragile ecosystems nourished by the bogs trump all. The balance between the two remains precarious.

●●●

Though the park officials have tried to cultivate a pre-industrial farmland as best they can, in places you can still see the crumbs of help left out for the still-vulnerable partridge. Most obvious are the feeders; white plastic silos, ringed in wire to keep larger herbivores from accessing the food they contain. In the centre of the conservation area there are hutches, in which as-yet-unreleased birds are stored in safety.

As the mid-afternoon heat swelters, unimpeded by a cloudless sky, a quad bike with two passengers rumbles along the trail that encircles the conservation area. It turns in across the field and grinds to a halt by the hutches. The passengers disembark and start to feed the partridges within. In their excitement, the partridges rise and fall like popcorn bursting from the heat. I'm tempted to get closer, if only for a better look. But the prospect of inspecting a caged partridge falters when compared to the thrill of finding a wild bird, and so I press on across the bog.

In my conceit, I had assumed that wild partridges would be easy to come by in so confined a space, afraid to abandon Boora for the lawless space beyond, with its rats and buzzards and foxes. Rounding every bend in the path, every patch of legumes, every dried rash of grass, I'd expect a partridge to go scurrying off. Perhaps the partridge, their senses sharpened by millions of years of avoiding being trampled underfoot, have heard my clumsy exploration of their domain coming, and retreated to dense cover from which even their bold orange heads cannot be seen. Or perhaps, eager to regain lost ground, they have poured out into the surrounding fields from whence the Reconquista, brood after brood, one field at a time, can commence, and once more the fields of the midlands might crawl with partridges.

Reed-fringed, the shores of a lake emerge from between low trees. Its water is like milk in the grey light, as I feel tender drips of rain start to caress my face. Above me, a storm cloud brews. Out on the surface of the water, a fleet of whooper swans floats gracefully into view. They are supreme in their domain, dwarfing the coots, mallards and little grebes that hug the reed beds around them. The weather may be turning. But you get the feeling this is a last stand of a cornered winter, a final foray over the trench to reclaim territory long lost to the advancing spring. The whoopers are the winter's advance guard, seizing a toehold as the rain clouds advance like an aerial armada.

But loyalties are fleeting. All of a sudden, as if seized by a sudden impulse to depart for breeding grounds in Iceland, the whoopers start pounding the water's surface as they struggle to take wing. They make an almighty percussion as they tear across the lake before finally, with much exertion, powering into the air.

The whoopers, like the other migrant birds that spend part of their year here, symbolise the ever-shifting birding profile of Lough Boora, arriving and departing with much fanfare. My elusive partridge, on the other-hand, vacillating from hedgerow to field year-round, is the omnipresent, unshakable presence at the Lough. Often hidden, never ostentatious, but always there, even if now only with benevolent intervention.

The flight home for the whoopers is a non-stop journey across the tempestuous North Atlantic, a phenomenal feat by any stretch. Perhaps this is it. Or perhaps they have tired of this body of water, and have set off on reconnaissance to find a more secluded space, with richer forage with which to stock up for longer travels ahead.

Regardless, they strike a handsome sight as they sail in a loose line, low over the bog.

RED GROUSE

The Military Road

When starting this book, I'd envisioned each target bird awaiting me at the end of a long journey, the pot of gold where the rainbow meets the ground. This was not to be one of those days.

No sooner had Mark, Austin and I left the car, and begun to make our way on foot along the smooth new road paved through the Wicklow Mountains, than I caught sight of a small, round head poking up through the long grass: my first red grouse.

Names can be deceiving. I'd trained myself to look for the russet-red grouse of field guides. This, however, is a female. She's almost as tan as the scorched grass she moves through. She disappears in and out of the mounds of grass studding the slope, blending in seamlessly. Scurrying along, more mammal than bird, she never hints at taking to the wing. Nor does she want to. Her energies can be put to better use up here. Every few steps, she halts to crane her head skyward, keeping us in view through the strands of grass and heather. Her progress is steady, almost waddling.

Then, fiddling with the camera, I take my eye from the prize. And she's gone.

Not gone. Just there, but hidden among the heather. There's no burst of wings as she beats for an escape. Instead, she lets her feathers melt her into the mountainside. We quarter the slope with our binoculars for any heads that might periscope up through the vegetation. But there's no sign of her, no neck raised to betray her presence, no cackling to break the silence. Frustrated, we take a seat on an embankment beside a small stream trickling down the slope. We're confident that her movement will give her away, that the fear that freezes her will subside, and she'll resume her business.

It doesn't happen. Spread out before us is a potpourri of browned grass, matted heather and boulders coloured by lichens. The grass, as if trying to fortify itself against the heather, is arranged in clumps. It makes shapes like small mountains peppering the slope. Behind any one a grouse could be crouching. And this slope is just one of many, each bleeding into the next as part of the massive Wicklow Mountain chain. But there are grouse here. Our fortuitous sighting, however brief, has confirmed that. So we set off once more, in hopes of a closer look.

●●●

The Wicklow Mountains have long been a holdout for the clandestine – both man and bird. It was to here that dissidents would come once expelled from the more fertile lowlands, here to lick their wounds, nurse their grudges and strike out for revenge.

These slopes were once the stronghold of Gaelic tribes in medieval times, the O'Tooles and O'Byrnes, who had been forced out of neighbouring Kildare by the hated Normans.

From here, they would launch vindictive raids against towns and estates as far afield as Dublin, taking livestock, silver and other booty back with them. In governmental records from the time, the mountains of what is now Wicklow (the county wasn't shired until 1606) are referred to as the *terre guerre* ('land of war') in contrast to the *terre pacis* ('land of peace') along the coast. A tit-for-tat of attack and counter-attack waged throughout the thirteenth and fourteenth centuries. The Black Castle in my native Wicklow Town stands as grim testimony to the carnage, burned by the O'Byrnes in 1295, 1301 and again in 1315.

Although the Anglo-Norman settlers were able to mobilise large forces in an effort to meet the rebels head on, the mountains themselves presented a formidable barrier to conquest and a decisive victory remained elusive. Even well-prepared armies would meet with calamity in the mountains. The problem escalated to such a degree that King Richard II was forced to intervene. He brought with him the largest invading force ever seen in medieval Ireland. Among his targets were the redoubtable clans of the mountains, the *Hibernici inimici* ('Irish enemies'). Devastated by the English archers, the mountain chiefs finally submitted in 1395.

Old habits die hard; the *terre guerre* would remain a lawless place, and a hotbed of insurrection, for many years to come. The O'Byrnes would not be parted from their power base in the mountains. In 1580 another scion of the family, Fiach McHugh, won a famous victory over an English army at Glenmalure. This was one of the worst defeats a British force would ever suffer in Ireland – and once again, the native Irish used their mastery of the mountainous terrain to win the day. In their wake, they left hundreds of English dead: 'a stream of Saxon gore', as recalled in the traditional Irish song 'Follow Me Up to Carlow'.

Centuries later, the rebels of 1798 would reprise the tradition of their Gaelic forebears, hiding out in the mountains to harass government forces by stealth. They would make this a perilous region right up until the early nineteenth century. It was to combat these rebels that the road we drove to get here came into being. Its purpose: to help crush the dissidents who fought on after the dream of 1798 had been scuttled. The route was cut through the mountains by the government of the day, creating an artery through which British soldiers could travel and rid the mountains of rebels.

In so doing, they also created what would become one of the most scenic drives in the county. At times both bleak and breathtaking, the Military Road (as it's still called) snakes its way up the Wicklow Mountains. It begins in south Dublin (Rathfarnham) and runs for nearly sixty kilometres down to Aughavannagh, buttressed by old barracks at Glencree, Laragh, Glenmalure and the Glen of Imaal. Along the way, it dips through bogs that in places peel back lairs of blackened peat, a record of the flora that thrived here long ago. The mountain slopes are covered with a patina of heather and grasses, tanned by the sun. The same sun takes a harder toll on the chalky, petrified wood of the shrubs foolhardy enough to attempt a living this high up. Many have been reduced to twisted, skeletal figures. They keep company with others who've succumbed, forming their own headstones in cemeteries grasping at the road. As it traces the contours of the slopes, the road rises to reveal vistas of distant mountaintops. Some are worn down to their granite and quartzite bedrock, others handsomely crowned with conifer plantations.

These days, as in Wicklow's violent past, more benign recluses call these mountains home. Red grouse are birds of these vast, often desolate spaces. Like all grouse, they are birds of mountains. They're the only grouse species we have left following the extinction of the capercaillie, a huge and magnificent bird that could not survive the forest clearances that swept through Ireland in centuries past. Across the Irish Sea, Britain also has the black grouse (another bird of the trees) and the ptarmigan (famed for its white winter coat, and confined to the highest peaks of Scotland). But amongst the heather-coated uplands of Ireland, only the red grouse resides, the lone ambassador of its clan. They and heather go together. The grouse live among the heather, sustain themselves from it, nest in it and hide within it when danger is close.

Islands that have been isolated for long periods often boast their own unique fauna that has slowly diverged from that of the neighbouring landmass. Mauritius, for instance, was cut adrift in the Indian Ocean long enough for a waylaid pigeon to lose the power of flight and evolve into the dodo. Ireland, however, has had no such stint of solitude long enough to develop its own unique cast of avian characters. We have only been separated from Britain since the end of the last Ice Age less than twelve thousand years ago, and so our wildlife has not been cast away for long enough to take off in its own evolutionary direction. Some of our species, however, are showing the first signs of embarking down that route. Our dippers, coal tits and jays are all recognised as unique races, separate from their British and continental cousins. And our red grouse is sometimes counted among that cohort too.

The bird we call the red grouse is actually the British and Irish counterpart of the continental willow ptarmigan. This species blends the rufous feathering of our grouse with the flecks of white needed to hide on high, snow-dusted slopes. Furthermore, the red grouse found in Ireland are generally lighter than their cousins in Britain.

This is thought to help them assimilate better into grassy slopes as well as heather, and has been cited as a reason why it deserves subspecies status, with *hibernicus* added to its title.

Indeed, it is plumage alone that separates the red grouse from the willow ptarmigan, which turns white in winter where the red grouse does not. The white is an adaptation to the kind of Alpine slopes we don't have in Ireland, and so in spaces where extensive, lasting snow cover is a rarity, the bird can maintain the same uniform year-round.

Defining new species is notoriously tricky; the Scottish crossbill was only recognised as a distinct species in 2006, on account of its song. The demarcation between race, subspecies and species adds to the confusion. Our race of dipper, for instance, is distinguished by the brown band on its chest, a trait not shared by dippers elsewhere. Our coal tits are unique in having a yellowish tinge. And Ireland's jay – one of the most striking birds we have – has diverged enough from other populations to warrant subspecies status, due to some slight adjustments in its genome over the millennia to make it better suited to life in Ireland's once vast oak forests.

Research indicates that the Irish red grouse population is indeed genetically distinct. This makes it all the more urgent that they get the protection they need. Analysis has also revealed shockingly low genetic diversity amongst red grouse here. This is due in no small part to the erosion of their highland habitat. The result? The enclaves of red grouse left are genetic islands, bottlenecks stranded throughout our various mountain ranges. Highly sedentary, these shrinking cohorts of grouse are cut adrift from outsiders that could inject new blood into the population. A lack of genetic diversity could leave them vulnerable to all the maladies inbreeding entails, such as low immunity and an inability to adapt to an ever-changing world.

●●●

In such a ubiquitous space as the mountainside can seem, you would think there's nothing to separate one patch of a few square metres from another. But such distinctions are singularly clear to the grouse. The cocks expend tremendous energies every autumn through spring, staking claim to the best real estate, and then holding it against all comers in the hope of enticing a mate.

It is now, in springtime, when the males are at their most belligerent. Like elephants entering musth, their bodies become flushed with testosterone to fuel the aggression needed to hold a prime territory. But unlike the open, leaking glands on the sides of an elephant's head, a male grouse's carnal desire manifests in more colourful ways. The red 'combs' above each of his eyes brighten, their resplendence reflecting his fitness and suitability for fatherhood. These licks of paint are among the most eye-catching plumage accents you'll find on any Irish bird. And they are as alluring to the females as they are to mountaineering birders. It is this hallmark of good genetic potential, as well as an estate with stunning mountain vistas and plentiful heather, that seduces the females.

After the grouse consummate their romance, the female builds her nest among the heather, relying on its thick mass of branches to shield her eggs and chicks from avian predators circling above: the buzzards and corvids that so often frequent this mountainous domain, as well as the merlins that hunt here in spring and the peregrines which can take even adult grouse. Like so many birds, the chicks need a near constant protein infusion to nourish their rapid growth. The grubs and insects flicking out of dormancy on the warming mountain slopes find themselves scooped up in broad grouse bills to be brought back to the nest. This is the only carnivorous phase in the grouse's lifecycle, and even its prey is hunted among the heather. In this way, the heather nourishes the grouse from the egg to the end.

It is this dependence upon heather, like pandas with bamboo, that is proving the grouse's undoing. Over the centuries, much of Ireland's wild heather has been cut or burned away. This is depriving the red grouse of the food and cover they need.

In Wicklow's prehistoric past, Irish elk stags with antlers spanning twice the height of a man fought for control of their harems on slopes like these. Now, it's their more modest relatives that infest the mountains, boasting descent in varying degrees from our native red deer and the introduced sika. Robbed of wolves not long before the rebellion of 1798 broke out, the mountains have no natural means of keeping the deer in check. Wicklow is now reckoned to have more of them than any county in Ireland. Throughout much of the mountain chain, they share the slopes with sheep. Together, they form a voracious grazing machine that can decimate the tender shoots and flowers of young heather – the same heather the red grouse depends on.

The heather that escapes the batteries of ungulate teeth must face a more incendiary threat. It's a long-standing tradition of upland farming to periodically burn the heather, to keep it from spreading too far and also to infuse the soil with nutrients that can then nourish next season's forage. But in the dry conditions that so often result from a long, hot summer, controlling flames started with the best intentions is difficult. Grouse nests, eggs and chicks can be lost.

Grazing wasn't the only economic value that impoverished farmers drew from the mountainside. Peat – to warm the hearth, and for sale – has proved one of the more fruitful harvests from the Irish uplands. Heather shuns the richer soils of the lowlands in favour of the hardier substrate so often found in the mountains. But along with the peat went the shrinking pool of space the heather could grow on, and that the grouse could call home.

In more recent times, another obstacle has emerged, one that can be seen all around the Wicklow Mountains today. They might be useless for wheat or potatoes, but the conditions up here are ideal for imported conifers, hardened by harsher northern climates. In an age when many farmers face economic hurdles (the number of full-time farmers in Ireland continues to plummet) afforestation has proved a lucrative supplement to their income. This benefits some birds. The grouse are not among them. Heather cannot grow in the shadow of evergreen needles – in fact, for all its resilience, it cannot abide shade at all. So, as the manufactured forests advance like shield walls up the slopes of the mountains, the cowering heather is forced to retreat, taking the red grouse with it.

In many ways, the fate of the grouse has found itself intertwined with the changing fortunes of Ireland as a whole. In the early 1900s the grouse population was flourishing, nurtured and protected for hunting on grouse moors. Grouse found shelter on the estates of wealthy landowners, which were tended by gamekeepers. The grouse paid for this upkeep with only a small and manageable sacrifice of numbers each year. In exchange, they were largely kept safe from any natural predators that might do them harm, the foxes and raptors that fell fowl of a gamekeeper's shotgun.

Grouse hunting was a time-honoured tradition of rural Irish life, particularly amongst the gentry. Like other aristocratic pastimes, it had developed its own code of ethics over the years. Although instinct tells the grouse to cling to the ground, for the sake of good sport it was considered bad form to shoot a bird unless in flight; far better to test your marksmanship on a moving target.

The birds (particularly young ones) were renowned for their gamey taste. They yielded a much leaner meat than chickens, though still tender and easy on the palette. Reared in the wild (grouse do not tame easily, and so the best meat can only be sourced from wild birds) the leanness of a grouse's meat meant it often had to be larded to boost the flavour. Preparing the birds for eating was a gruesome process, as Nancy Jackman, who worked as a cook for a number of British aristocratic families in the early twentieth century, reveals in her book *The Cook's Tale*:

> When the grouse came in August and September we had to leave them hanging for a couple of weeks in a cool room that had air coming into it from outside ... You knew then they were ready because maggots would be dropping off them in a steady stream. Unless you've cleaned – that is, gutted – a really rotten grouse you can have no idea of the stomach-churning smell. Very few people can do it without retching – even if they do it outside in the fresh air ... Apart from the maggots, their guts would also often be full of what looked like tapeworms – and the worms were

still alive. I used to think, if that's a delicacy, you can keep it.

Maintaining grouse moors was (and is) an art form unto itself, honed over centuries like any animal husbandry practice. As well as keeping predators and advancing forests in check, the gamekeeper must also take meticulous care of the heather, keeping it at the right length to provide shelter for the birds while also ensuring the estate was stocked with plants of all ages. The heather had to be pared back and burnt with precision, cultivating a microclimate in which montane insects could thrive. This would guarantee a steady food source for grouse chicks each spring. And if the grouse grew so fond of this human-tended oasis as to overpopulate it, the gamekeeper would then be called upon to play the role of raptor, culling their numbers just enough to stabilise the population.

But the Irish independence struggle that tore the country apart from 1916 until 1922 would see drastic changes in Ireland's landholding structure – and a decline in the grouse's fortunes as a result. The large country estates of the mainly Anglo-Irish aristocracy came under renewed attack from Republicans, both during the War of Independence and the civil war that followed. Around two hundred were burnt out between 1920 and 1923. With fewer affluent landowners to pay for their upkeep, many of the former grouse moors kept by the retreating aristocratic class were dissolved into smaller farm holdings. Deprived of gamekeepers, the moors fell victim to grazing, turf cutting and afforestation.

Together, these factors have taken their toll on the grouse of the Wicklow Mountains. The story is the same across many of Ireland's upland areas, with the grouse population falling by as much as 60 per cent in just thirty years. Recent surveys have shown no halt to this alarming trend. Small wonder, then, that the species has been the focus of intense conservation concern in recent years.

●●●

As we tread our way through the heather, I sympathise with the rebels who once made their hideout here. I can even spare a thought for the armies who floundered on these slopes trying to destroy them. Unlike the tender-feathered shoes of the grouse, bulky human feet were not meant to master such terrain. When my boot does find sure footing on the uneven surface it's often at an angle, causing me to stumble. The grass may be scorched, but it still shields the ground below from the sun. Now, the heather and grass clumps conceal the swampy soil beneath, carpeted with damp moss. You can sink up to your knees into it if you're not careful – to say nothing of the incessant incline. Advancing into battle – or running for your life – up here could not have been easy.

Mark makes easier progress through the mass of heather. He knows the uplands well, having spent time up here fulfilling the role of predator left vacant by the long-dead wolves. With nothing to control the deer, hunters have had to take their place. At certain times of year, quotas for stags and hinds have to be met to keep the population in check, and try to restore a more natural balance to the uplands.

Mark loves the wildlife of the mountains. He knows the best places from which to watch the stags during the autumn rut. I've been up here with him before to see and photograph the spectacle. They string out across valley floors, taking up places like prostitutes claiming their own portion of a street. From here they issue long, mournful whistles to lure in herds of does.

He knows the best places because he's been here to hunt the deer before. But to him, the culling is a necessary evil. He takes pride in the fact that none of the deer he's hunted have been left to rot, disposed as toxic waste. Instead, the meat provided a feast for friends and family. I can accept the utility of this, as well as the good that culling the deer can do for the landscape – and for the grouse.

The trees, though, are a more imposing adversary. Tired from our exertions up the mountainside, we slump into the heather to rest. To our left, a vast line of conifers looms, like soldiers marching up the slope, nothing to impede them save three tiring travellers looking for grouse. Within their tightly-packed ranks I can just about discern the forest floor, threadbare and dead. The soil beneath has been sapped of nutrients by the ruthless roots of the conifers. With so little light penetrating even on such a bright day, it makes for a grim domicile that few native creatures (much less the grouse) can readily inhabit.

Thankfully, the natural vegetation still holds its own for now. Grouse relish the seclusion up here. While the high mountains of Europe can harbour the occasional oasis of life, in Ireland the uplands can so often be a barren expanse. Few birds can find the food they need among the heather. Every once in a while, we see a meadow pipit perched on a boulder. Overhead, a trio of ravens chase each other, wheeling across the sky, guttural caws heralding their arrival. And in the late afternoon, as the clouds recede, a buzzard starts to circle, blending into the blue halfway through the circuit, only to reappear with each turn.

As we make our way back to the slope on which we first saw the grouse, the lack of cloud cover overhead exposes us to remorseless rays of sun. Even in March, it feels gloriously bright and hot. It's the kind of light that can craft things of beauty even out of desolation, like the petrified skeleton of a bush overlooking a twinkling stream. Its greying remains are lit up in vivid silver. The outlines of the crevices crawling up its trunk and limbs supply the contrast.

My feet are soon overheating in my climbing boots. Ignoring the age-old wisdom of mountaineers, I kick them off to embrace the relief of the damp moss beneath me. Easing back into the heather, curling my toes into the carpet of the mountain, I let inquisitive ants explore my boots in droves. The buzzard above keeps watch on our little party before circling off down the mountainside.

Following it with our eyes, we see the slopes of the Wicklow Mountains rising and falling to the horizon. It's as if they're reaching for some unseen treasure in the sky, faltering at every attempt and mounting another grab for glory, each failure imprinted on the landscape. Trees clump on their slopes in patches, like mounds of skin peeling from some great moulting animal. But up here, it's the heather that truly dominates. That great domain of the red grouse stretches like a blanket, following the contours of the mountains, colouring them rufous wherever the greys of granite and quartzite can't punch through.

The rebels had it hard here. But perhaps, between hunger, cold and grievances old, they found succour in this grim beauty.

CORNCRAKE

Tory Island

The frustration is agonising.

The field in front of me is barely an acre in size, hemmed in by barbed wire on all sides. Spread out across its surface are buttercups in full bloom, overshadowed by nettles and the occasional thistle. Orchids add a dash of pink here and there, and the white of the bog cotton is like little clumps of snow from a winter long past. Silverweeds lend a ghostly glow to this mosaic of colour. Black rushes stand in furrows, curved over by brown bags of seeds close to the tips.

It's scant shelter for any bird to hide in. There are no hedges, shrubs or trees in which they can take shelter; the soil is too shallow to anchor them, too poor to nourish their growth.

But through it all, my quarry eludes every scan of the space in front of me. Its distinctive call, a rasping bark unlike any bird cry I've heard before, echoes around the surround.

It's so close you'd swear you could touch it. And yet my eyes can't find my target. At times it seems closer and further away, mocking me, making use of secret tunnels through the field to circumvent my surveillance. Wheatears and meadow pipits bounce from post to post, doing everything they can to distract my gaze. But I stay focussed on the sound, and its maker that I cannot see.

The croaking continues. But by now, the light has turned against me. Swallows alight on the barbed wire to rest after a long day pursuing insects on the wing. The rambunctious starlings and tree sparrows that swarm over the surrounding outhouses have begun to calm. The natural rhythm of the night is setting in. And I can feel my body clock falling in line, a long day's travel taking its toll. I turn away from the field and strike off down the road. Perhaps magnanimous in eluding my detection, or just saving its breath for later, the corncrake stops calling.

●●●

This is the farthest north in Ireland I've ever come to find a bird. In fact, it's almost as far north as Ireland goes. Below me, the boat rocks in rhythm with the waves, the sea a murky black. The sky above is a textured, furrowed grey. And where they meet sits Tory Island, nine miles off the coast of Donegal.

As the boat swings in a loop around Inishbofin, Tory (as it's called locally) slowly materialises out of the North Atlantic. The lighthouse, rising proud out of the sea, is the first giveaway. The west side of the island appears flat and gentle, the east side bulbous and steep (save a u-shaped cleft in the middle). Three ridges of rock bisect the centre, like the crests of waves.

As you draw closer the houses come into view, like herds of sheep dotting a slope. They are grouped into two loose towns, one to the east and one to the west. There's not a tree in sight to obscure the view.

I first noticed this idiosyncrasy of Ireland's Atlantic isles on the Aran Islands of County Galway many years ago. Coming from such a forested county as Wicklow, the dearth of trees was almost unnerving. The karst landscape – a network of natural trenches hollowed out of the limestone – left soil of scarce depth to support large trees. What shrubs there were of shoulder height or higher were often withered and pitiful.

Tory doesn't have karst. But the wild Atlantic breezes and thin soil also make it next to impossible for trees to take root. As a result, a catalogue of tree-dwelling birds you'd take for granted on the mainland never colonised Tory; robins and thrushes are noteworthy for their absence, ditto rooks, jackdaws and magpies. But instead, the island (home to fewer than two hundred people) offers sanctuary to a host of ground-nesting species: the oystercatchers, wheatears and pipits who weave their nests in the grass or refurnish an abandoned rabbit hole.

Of all these inhabitants there's one for which Tory is especially renowned. It's become somewhat of a holy grail among Irish birders, given the dramatic (and tragic) decline it's undergone over the last century. From being an integral part of the fabric of the Irish summer, it's been largely reduced to a few rocky outposts on the north and west coasts. The corncrake.

Given that the usual songsters of summer are altogether absent from Tory, I was expecting a vacuum of avian silence upon disembarking in West Town. How wrong I was. Tracing my way along the streets, around the small, white-washed chapel, a cacophony of bird noise fills the air. The irritated babble of tree sparrows follows me as I circle the church. They're another species that has found special sanctuary on Tory, where their bulkier cousin the house sparrow has yet to gain a foothold. Further out in the fields there's the *zeet* of lapwings, rising from the grass to steer herring gulls away from their nests. Starling chicks crown wooden fence posts, begging for grubs from devoted parents. And a wheatear flicks from perch to perch, his beak whiskered with the legs and wings of crane flies, doing a circuit of his territory before returning to the nest.

Then, amidst it all, I hear it; the cry I've come so far to hear. The closest thing I can compare it to is someone crudely raking a stick against a güiro, twice in quick succession, the second note a slightly higher pitch than the first. It's far from the most attractive sound in the bird world. There's almost an automation in the rhythm of it, more like a mechanical malfunction than the rich repertoire of vocal flourishes you might expect from farmland birds. But it's nothing if not potent. It travels far in its brutal, hoarse simplicity, the aftertaste like a football being pounded against a brick wall.

Long bouts of calling are interrupted by lengthy pauses, frustrating my urge to zero in on a corncrake garden or field. The audio-space is filled once more by the sounds of the more familiar birds. I start to discern a corncrake's croak in the *tsshing* of young starlings and even the distant honks of gulls. At times I have to physically stop, motionless, so as to pick out a corncrake when it resumes calling among the chatter, a meditation to re-centre my search.

Eventually I track one to a field at the back of some houses. Another male has staked his claim to the field next to his. I notice that when one starts calling, the other soon resumes his song as well, fearing that a rival left unchallenged will garner all the affections of the females that sojourn in silence through the daffodils and nettles.

Male corncrakes can sing like this for much of the day because they're unencumbered by the fatherly duties of many other birds. Parenting is usually the province of the female corncrake; she alone incubates the eggs and feeds the chicks. The male's role is to locate a prime spot in the undergrowth from which to call incessantly, drawing all the females within earshot to him to mate. The strength and vigour of his call is the sole measure of his worth. As I listen, I wonder what endears the females to such a blunt, unattractive sound. Clearly the health of a male corncrake, his suitability as a progenitor, is writ large in his croak, the vessel of a rich aural tapestry beyond the scope of human hearing.

For all their vocal prowess, corncrakes are notoriously shy. The males prefer to call from deep cover, buried in the undergrowth. It is this that comes between me and my first corncrake sighting on my first day on Tory. With a weary head I retreat to bed, hoping tomorrow will bring better fortune.

•••

Although not blessed with the same profusion of ruins as some of Ireland's better-known islands, there are still glimpses of Tory's past to be found, in a round tower collapsed on one side and sites like the West Town's Church of the Seven. This tiny chapel, the size of a double bed, has been worn almost down to its foundations over the years, although its emaciated western wall still stands in a triangle.

Behind it, the Grave of the Seven is marked by a rusted Celtic cross. It's named after the seven people (six men and a woman) who were supposedly buried here in a time long passed, drowned at sea, once a common death for residents of Ireland's Atlantic islands. The clay on the grave still looks chocolate brown and fresh. According to legend, it's much prized for its ability to keep seafaring vessels free of rats. These properties also apply to the island as a whole;

Tory is devoid of rodents, another reason why it's such an ideal sanctuary for ground-nesting birds, among them the corncrake.

As if through gratitude to the deeds of the seven, a corncrake starts calling in the thick undergrowth that spreads out around the church. I crouch down and peer out over the remains of the walls like a sentry risking a lookout over the trench. I scan every nettle leaf and thistle spine for a glimpse of the corncrake it might conceal. But the frustration of yesterday resumes. The breeze swirling in from the Atlantic sends shivers through the nettles. Through my binoculars, I hope in vain that every twitch in the plants will betray a corncrake moving through them. But no bird comes stumbling out.

Instead the pattern is the same. The corncrake calls on and off, relentlessly trying to outdo the males in the field across the road. Each bout of croaking seems to come from a different spot in the field. Perhaps the bird is moving from base to base to lay claim to the whole field. Perhaps he's trying to widen his catchment area of females by enveloping as much space as possible, or simply trying to find the best spot from which to project his call across the island. It amazes me how he can move about so seamlessly through the nettles, thistles and daffodil fronds without detection, much less be croaking within two metres of me and still go unseen. Were it not for the call, you'd be none the wiser that one of Ireland's rarest birds was right in front of you, probably staring you in the face.

I turn to the field across the road to see how his rivals are performing. There are two males calling here, begrudgingly sharing a larger space between them. One is right in front of me, *crek crek*-ing from deep within a ball of nettles. Whenever he starts, his rival is not long taking up the challenge. At times, their calls fall comically out of sync with each other, a shambolic duet deaf to tone and timing, only to fall back into rhythm and blend together with a redoubled potency.

Then, at last, I see it. Towards the northwest corner of the field, where the nettles and daffodils start to thin out and give way to grass and licks of silverweed, the face of a corncrake melts out of my binoculars. He's braving the open to call out in the morning sun, as if defying his rival to abandon the safety of the nettles.

Bathed in light and set adrift amid the green sheen of the grass, at last I get a chance to study his form. Corncrakes are distant cousins of coots and moorhens; subtract the facial shield and lobed feet and adjust the colours and the resemblance is clear. They're about the length of a blackbird, though far bulkier; he appears almost jackdaw sized, with a long neck widening into a pot belly. Orange and grey converge along his head and neck, beginning to bar beneath the wings. His bold, spotted back is almost completely hidden. He tosses his head skyward with each croak, revealing the pink mouth as his dark eyes flash grey.

He can't be more than ten metres away from me. Yet he takes no notice and makes no dash for cover. For a bird that clung so tenaciously to cover before, he shows no fear out in the open. He remains steadfast at the same spot, the silverweed and grass fanning out around him. He turns ever so slightly with each bout of calling, maybe to project his voice in another direction and entice mates from a different corner of the field. A single male may have several females breeding within his territory, laying, incubating and tending to her brood, all in silence, inconspicuous, while the male draws as much attention to himself as possible. It's quite a thought to imagine a whole coterie of corncrakes of all ages, from hatchlings to hardened veterans of winter sojourns to Africa, all hidden from sight amongst the nettles.

Without a father to help them, and only having a short summer window in which to mature, corncrake chicks are precocious. It only takes them five weeks to fledge, at which point they're ready to cross continents as the weather turns. While many of their counterparts remain nest-bound for weeks, the black, downy young of the corncrake are following their mother around the fields of Tory within days, and can become fully independent of her within just two weeks. In this timeframe, she'll stock them up with the protein needed to fire their rapid growth, picking off insects, arachnids, slugs and even the defenceless chicks of other birds unfortunate enough to cross her path.

I'm overcome with relief at seeing the male. Over the last day on the island, I'd become resigned to the frustration that awaited me, hearing corncrakes right in front of me but never seeing one. I had waited by the Church of the Seven for well over an hour for one of the three males calling within its orbit to show his face. And now that one has, the sighting, as is so often the case with a bird you've waited so long to see, is brief. A quick glance at my phone, a foolish concession to modern life, and he's gone. Head down, silent, slinking away into the nettles.

An old islander comes sauntering up the road behind me. White bucket and spade in hand, his red face is smeared with sunscreen. We exchange pleasantries; noticing my binoculars and long lens, he knows I've come to the island for corncrakes.

'There's plenty of them about,' he says. 'Ah, sure, you don't get them everywhere nowadays.'

●●●

You certainly don't.

Once, the cry of the corncrake could be heard right across Ireland. It was still a confirmed breeder in all Irish counties right up until the early '70s'. My grandfather used to hear them call in the fields around Bray as a young man. But this fair-weather sound likely hasn't been heard on a Wicklow farm in my lifetime. Such is the terrible impact simple changes can have on creatures that need specific conditions to flourish.

Its presence was as integral to the summer experience in rural Ireland as the swallow's is to this day. For generations, the call of the corncrake was a sign of warm days ahead. The bird has woven its way into Ireland's poetic anthology. In 'A Song of the Tan War', it forms part of the tapestry of rural Limerick. The Shannon was once the bird's stronghold on mainland Ireland. It was here also that flying columns killed (or were killed) during the War of Independence:

On the sod in Ballyroe.
The lark will sing at morn's break,
O'er the spot where Sean Finn died,
The cuckoo and the corncrake
Will be there at eventide;
And when summer's rose in fragrance blows,
And through winter's frost and snow,
His memory shall ever be
Revered round Ballyroe

This piece makes reference to a famed eccentricity of the corncrake: its penchant for singing at dusk. It's as if the bird, knowing that it's monotonous 'cack' cannot compete with the litany of florid warbles stemming from the passerines, has to wait for radio silence before taking centre stage.

The beautiful inefficiency of horse and plough, of hoe and hand, left it with plenty of space to breed in safety. Sustenance farming suited the bird – literally down to the ground. When farmers had no one but their own families to feed, and perhaps a local market to sell to, the land could be worked at a rhythm that was benevolent to visiting corncrakes.

Those days are a distant memory. For the last half-century or more, metal and wheels have wrought a greater profit from the Irish farm, at a terrible cost to the corncrake. Earlier, more vigorous cutting (for the purpose of silage, not haymaking) fell out of sync with the bird's breeding cycle. Chicks and nests were ravaged season after season by combine harvesters. Grasslands meticulously managed for livestock fell out of the corncrake's favour.

Even if the farmland were to be left at the mercy of nature, and the natural foliage allowed to return unchecked, this would only favour the corncrake to a point. This is not a species that can thrive in dense bush, the kind of wiry woodland habitat that would inevitably coat much of Ireland were civilisation to retreat. Instead, it prefers open spaces, but with just enough cover from which to call and nest in safety. Pre-modern farming methods provided that in abundance. In twenty-first-century Ireland it's in tragically short supply.

And so are corncrakes.

It's perhaps no coincidence that the corncrake has gone much the way of the Irish language in recent decades. Their ranges overlap to a remarkable degree, both of them largely relegated to enclaves along the north and west coasts. (In some good summers, corncrakes can also establish a bridgehead in the Midlands, though this is now tragically rare.) Despite the islander's assertion, there aren't plenty of corncrakes around – even here in its Donegal citadel the bird is not as numerous as it once was. True, recent surveys have revealed an encouraging uptick in numbers: an increase of 8 per cent to 151 calling males. But this is far from the ubiquitous presence they once had across the Irish countryside each summer.

My first exposure to the corncrake came while leafing through Irish birdwatching magazines as a child. Together with the barn owl, it always seemed like *the* bird in the most trouble, the one that most needed saving.

Its decline is more tragic because this is not a bird that needs a vast wilderness separating it from the influence of man; it can happily thrive within feet of human habitation, as proven by the males calling proudly from the back gardens of Tory. Given how vital the island is to the survival of the species in Ireland, many of the locals have been paid to let their gardens and fields return to the natural state in which corncrakes can flourish.

Today, it breeds only in places where the apparatus of conventional farming can get no purchase in the shallow, rocky soil. Just such a spot is Tory Island.

●●●

The conditions that make Tory so ideal for corncrakes have made it a tough outpost for human habitation for centuries. Exposed, and with no trees to offer any protection, the island is at the mercy of the North Atlantic throughout the worst of the winter. Even today, its supply line to the mainland is occasionally severed by unnavigable winter swells.

Living here required that you be cut from tougher cloth than the more bucolic life on the mainland. The islanders of old were renowned as a hardy breed. They clung on in houses with low roofs and soft edges that left nothing for gusts to grab on to. As precious little could be grown on the island, and without the space to tend large herds of livestock, many of them put out to sea to make a living. In such tempestuous waters, many did not return.

More still took a boat to more prosperous nations and never returned. In so doing, they wrote another chapter in the long, tragic history of emigration from Ireland's impoverished west coast. With it went much of the lifeblood of the Irish language, and the Gaelic culture nourished on these rugged coasts for millennia. It pains me to think what songs, poems and yarns might have been lost to memory, no one still living to recall them, and no one at the time with the forethought to write them down. Some survive though, and can still be heard in the traditional *ceilí*s, the Irish set dances so integral to Gaeltacht life.

The island's relationship with the mainland has long been as rocky as its soil. In the Celtic tradition, Tory was the stronghold of the Fomorians, a demonic race who antagonised the angelic Tuatha dé Danann that dwelt on the mainland. Their leader was Balor, a monstrous cyclops who could incinerate his enemies with fire from his one eye. His legend mirrors that of the island-dwelling Polyphemus of Homer's *Iliad*. Balor, though, would meet an even more tragic end at the hands of his own grandson, Lugh. Fearing his daughter, Eithne, would bear the son prophesied to destroy him, Balor kept her locked away in a tower on the east end of the island. Nevertheless, by the machinations of a local man, Eithne would give birth to a son, Lugh. It was Lugh, with the help of the blacksmith of the Tuatha dé Danann, who would bring an end to the tyrannical Balor, driving a spear through his head at the base of Mount Errigal.

Mainlanders long saw Tory as a place to come to invoke the supernatural; walking around the island before three successive sunrises, praying at its holy sites along the way before turning a sacred stone, would bring misfortune upon your enemies. Many shipwrecks in the area would be attributed to this procedure. The *Cloch na Mallacht*, or cursing stone, was hidden in the late nineteenth century to prevent a repeat of the incident that sank HMS *Wasp* off the island in 1884, taking fifty-two sailors with it.

These days, Tory is at peace. Peace is the ideal word to describe a walk around the island. The laidback lifestyle it now offers is evident in the couples taking in Atlantic views from their front gardens, in every islander you pass greeting you with a 'hello' or a wave from their driver's seat. The low houses that once held fast against the wind have been mostly replaced by more modern structures, many whitewashed but others in bolder colours of yellow, orange, red and pink, with slated roofs and crumbling, corrugated outhouses. The local patter emanating from the houses is so thick it can be hard to tell if it's English or Irish. But you can still see touches of an Irish life fast fading here, even in simple things like clothes hung from a long chord stretched between wooden posts, and walls of piled stone parting field from road.

As you head east from West Town, the verdant gardens that play host to singing corncrakes begin to thin out, and the no-man's land between the island's two settlements opens up in front of you. I hear one solitary male calling in a distant field; maybe he's having more joy than the duelling duos in West Town. Or maybe he's the romantic dud, relegated to the outskirts from the more desirable property in the town itself. I'll never know.

The further east I walk along the island's one road, the more the soil becomes thread bare, worn down by centuries of exposure to the North Atlantic wind. It gives way to pale grey limestone, like scabs criss-crossing the surface of the island.

Tory is tiny. It doesn't take long to venture as east as east goes. The east end of the island rises sharply out of the sea, connected to the rest of Tory by a dipping sliver of stone. The coves on either side provide sheltered bays for cormorants and divers to fish in. The cliffs around me echo with the honks of gulls. Fulmars, stiff winged, occasionally circle into view. Choughs caw before alighting on a crumbling cliff face, the delicate red bill ready to pry a meal from the meagre soil.

Above me, the slope leading towards the highest cliff face ascends steeply, the surface gravelled with small, jagged stones. But nowhere is Tory without colour. Buttercups burst up from between the stone, yellowing the slope. Dotted between are pink dots of thrift, a flower that thrives within the embrace of the sea breeze. Combined, they make a perfect backdrop for the male wheatear following me up the slope in loops, seeing off any unwelcome visitor straying too close to his nest. Against the flourishing petals, his silver and black uniform is all the more striking.

I sit in blissful silence and stare away to the west. Here, almost as far north as Ireland goes, I can finally escape man-made noise. The view laid out before me is immense; small wonder Balor chose to construct his fortress here.

Below, Atlantic currents slither in geometric patterns across the surface of the sea. Overhead, the clouds that have followed me up and down the island are finally starting to break, setting the mountains and headlands of Donegal in a mosaic of light and towering shadow. Clearest among them is Errigal, that angular mass of silver rock where Balor met his end.

I wonder if, in a timeline lost to legend, he sat in this very spot, regarding the mainland with an envious eye, a hostile land ripe for conquest. As it was for him then, I hope it will be for the corncrake in the years to come. But with luck, and the benign neglect of man, this venture will encroach much further than the mountains of north Donegal.

Immersed in such serenity, I'd happily turn to stone sitting here. But the cruel conveniences of modern, scheduled living are all too close. The afternoon is wearing on. The boat that bore me to the island will soon again dock at the pier in West Town. The sea summons me home.

CUCKOO

Connemara

Companion in tow, I follow the crest of the ridge around Counshingaun. Around me, the Comeragh Mountains of County Waterford rise and fall, lending a dramatic edge to a countryside otherwise carved into mundane fields. It's a walk that takes you past lakes pooled into deep ravines and remote caves that once served as hideouts for bandits, proto-Robin Hoods who harassed travellers through the countryside and wove their way into local myth.

Our descent is overshadowed by ravens. Guttural croaks remind us of their presence. They wheel overhead in vigilant surveillance, black streaks against the blue of the lake below. Sheep spread out across the rough fields. Every now and then we happen across a lamb tucked in amongst the gorse. Hardier are the feral goats, horns long and coats matted with mud, skirts that sweep the ground as they run for cover. For the most part, I think it a dull place for birds, with nothing save the craneflies clawing like zombies out of the ground to sustain them.

Then, amid the silence that oozes into the valley, I hear it:

wuck-oo
wuck-oo
wuck-oo

Even if I knew nothing of bird calls, I'd know this one. It's without doubt the most recognisable of all Irish bird noises, a sound a novice could hear just once and pin to its maker.

The eponymous cry rises and falls across the landscape. In vein I inventory the stunted bushes and rotted wooden fence posts that divide the fields, hoping to see the cuckoo. Nowhere. And with such a simple call that can travel so far, there's no telling where in the mountains he is calling from. We push on, through copses of pines, for home.

●●●

This was the only time I'd ever heard a cuckoo call. On untold summer days of boyhood, a hope of hearing that call had lurked in the back of my mind. Many mornings, woken by the woodpigeons that roosted in the forest behind our house, I had imagined squeezing the bi-syllabic call of the cuckoo into the quintet-noted cry of the woodpigeon; ditto with the three-note burr of the collared dove. But the only cuckoos I would see as a child were the wooden contraptions that sprung from stately clocks in the countryside, crowning the hour with their calls. It was a synesthetic phenomenon, a sound I'd come to associate with mud-crusted wellingtons and stuffed animals mounted in hallways.

Even more so than that cry, the cuckoo is most famous for its extraordinary breeding cycle, a form of brood parasitism practiced by no other Irish bird. This is what first piqued my interest in the cuckoo. It flies in the face of the parenting instincts which most birds are known for; no other animals practice the degree of monogamous dual parenting seen amongst most birds. It's as if the cuckoos, acknowledging their underhanded nature and pitiful inadequacy as parents, are happy to surrender that most basic of duties to other birds. Or they are just glad to take advantage of their nurturing nature.

Flying about the farmland and moor, the female cuckoo zeroes in on the nest of a smaller species (in Ireland, typically a meadow pipit – indeed, the symbiotic bond between the two is so strong that the meadow pipit in Irish was called '*Banaltra na Cuaice*', the cuckoo's nurse). Passerines usually rotate incubation duties, but there are still brief windows when the nest is left completely unoccupied. It is in this opening that she must act. With an agility and dexterity perhaps surprising for her size, she scrambles on top of the fragile nest structure, swallows one of the eggs for good measure and deposits her own as fast as she can in its place. The returning meadow pipit (or reed warbler, or dunnock, or other hapless victim) is oblivious. I wonder is it just coincidence that the words 'cuckoo' and 'cuckold' are so close.

Cuckoos develop fast – and they need to. Despite almost always being laid after its new nest mates, the cuckoo's egg is usually the first to hatch. But for the chick, its work is just beginning. Naked and blind, but driven by a savage determination that can be disturbing to behold, the chick instantly begins prosecuting the demise of the unhatched eggs around it. Cradling them on its back, it uses its featherless wings to leverage them out of the nest, one by one, until every egg has crashed through the underbrush or sunk into the water beneath the reeds. With no sight to guide it, this macabre endeavour can take hours. But it has to be done.

You would think the host parents might be suspicious at the carnage below their nest, if not of the only chick to survive it. Not so. With the other chicks killed in their shells, the baby cuckoo is now the envy of hatchlings everywhere, the sole beneficiary of its new parents' affections. It alone gets to fatten up on the conveyer belt of grubs and flies ferried in by the parents. Its calorific demands alone are easily equal to a whole brood of pipit or warbler chicks, which is why it makes a point of dispatching them before they can eat into this supply. The hosts, blinded by loyalty to a chick hatched in their nest, are none the wiser. By now they have well and truly imprinted upon this alien entity they are raising.

The deception is aided by another weapon the young cuckoo comes equipped with: its call. The trills of the growing cuckoo chick are a perfect match for a whole brood of passerine hatchlings, compelling the parents to keep feeding it more and more. Even after the cuckoo's true form starts to reveal itself, and it begins to burst out of the delicate nest unsuited to a bird so large, the parent's devotion persists. By the time the juvenile cuckoo has rendered the very suspension of the nest around it, it receives its meals from the comfort of a branch or fence post. From here, it can begin to build its flight muscles for the long migration ahead, while still enjoying its parent's largesse. A pipit or warbler stuffing insects into the gaping maw of a chick now five times its size is surely one of the most perverse scenes in the entire bird world.

Every facet of the cuckoo's existence is designed to abet this bizarre breeding strategy, including its appearance. In adulthood, the bird is vaguely reminiscent of a raptor; its grey colouring matches that of the male sparrowhawk, and its outline (long tail, pointed wings) evokes a falcon. Very occasionally, a rufous-and-black morph will appear, but this scarcer cuckoo is no more encumbered, as its colouration is a mirror for a female kestrel.

Flying about, this profile elicits the instinctual responses that many prey species have to a raptor: they either rise from the undergrowth to mob it, or flee for their lives. In either case, they betray the locations of their nests to the female cuckoo, helping her to home in on her target. Raptorial mimicry comes with other advantages as well. For the sparrowhawk, a darker back helps conceal it in the undergrowth, and a barred stomach breaks up its outline, making it difficult to see from the front too. These traits work equally well for the female cuckoo, who also has need for stealth. And when cruising about in the open, predators that would otherwise be tempted to attack a relatively harmless cuckoo might refrain from challenging the more belligerent sparrowhawk. So the impersonation could even help keep the cuckoo safe; the illusion of danger, like the venom-free kingsnake or stingless hoverfly.

Even the egg of the cuckoo has a part to play in the great deception. For all their fawning over the new arrival in their nest, host parents will naturally attack an egg that is irrefutably alien. To combat this, cuckoos have evolved eggs that mimic those of their hosts, allowing them to slot into a nest undetected.

Remarkably, the colour of the egg varies from female to female, forcing her to parasite the nests of one particular species. The genes that determine egg colour stem solely from the female cuckoo; the male line has no say in the matter. This is critical. If a mated couple descend from different lines of egg specialists (the male from a mottled brown egg modelled on that of the reed warbler, the female from a sky-blue imitation of a dunnock's) and the egg colour of their offspring borrowed equally from both, it would not sufficiently mimic the colour and pattern of either species to execute the deception. The resultant hybrid-coloured egg would be instantly identified and discarded.

The imprinting between host and parasite flows both ways. Cuckoo hatchlings identify with the host species that raised them, and will target this species as hosts for their own offspring, perpetuating the parasitical cycle. This is another reason why cuckoos are loyal to the same breeding areas year-in, year-out; any deviation, and the female cuckoo might end up in a habitat where there are not enough hosts of the particular species for which she is adapted.

How brood parasitism – which seems so counterintuitive – first came into being remains unclear. It probably stemmed from birds that commandeered the nests of other species to lay their eggs in. Perhaps one of these nest pirates jumped the gun, depositing its clutch in a stolen nest before evicting the eggs of its owner. By fortuitous happenstance, the two clutches might have had similar patterning – and the nest builder, naïve to the manoeuvrings of this proto-cuckoo, saw no need for suspicion. When this nest builder then raised the chicks of the proto-cuckoo, reproduction by subterfuge was born.

I wonder if, perhaps, it goes back even further than that. We now know that feathers aren't the only inheritance bequeathed to the birds by their dinosaur forebears. All bird eggs to this day are coloured by combinations of just two pigments: blue-green biliverdin and red-brown protoporphyrin IX. These same pigments once decorated the eggs of the dinosaurs. Tied to terra firma, perhaps the nests of dinosaurs were also open to pre-avian brood parasites, and this strange chord in the long, diverse symphony of reproductive strategies, honoured by the ancestors of the cuckoo, followed the birds onto the wing, through the demise of the dinosaurs and into modern times. We'll probably never know.

While this lifestyle frees cuckoos from the constraints of parenting, it also leaves them at the mercy of their host's breeding cycle. Any shift in nesting patterns among pipits, warblers, wagtails and other hosts can see the cuckoo arriving too late to find nests of unhatched eggs in which to lay its own. Evidence suggests that some of the more common target species have, in more recent years, started to breed five or six days earlier in the year, knocking them out of tempo with the cuckoo's northward migration. This is one theory cited to explain the decline of the cuckoo, a decline we are yet to fully understand. In Ireland specifically, the cuckoo's reliance on the meadow pipit as a host could be its undoing. The meadow pipit breeds in upland heather and rough pasture, both of which have been in retreat for some time.

I would later learn that the east coast where I grew up is, in general, a poor spot for cuckoos. Unlike the pigeons and doves, the faux cuckoos calling outside my boyhood bedroom, this was not a bird to readily take to the suburbs. Instead, its penchant for wider, open countryside gave it a westerly bias; it is a creature of the Burren, a creature of Connemara. And Connemara is one striking place to spend a summer weekend.

●●●

It begins in Spiddal. Disembarking from the bus, the town's beach is festooned with crisping seaweed, wilting for want of the sea's embrace. This blemish is not enough to ward off the visitors, thronging the sand and seafront promenade. Further out, Galway Bay glistens like a field of blue glitter. The promenade brings back more boyhood memories: strolling its length with my family as the sun went down over the bay, the smell of periwinkles sold in brown paper cones.

Growing up, Spiddal played a small but important role in shaping my concept of Ireland. It was the first place I experienced a mass through Irish. This was with my mother during that same childhood holiday. The experience was surreal; all the rituals – the kneeling, the communion, the sign of peace – were identical. And yet the medium was so different, almost alien. This was the first time I came face to face with the duality of modern Ireland, of living, breathing, Irish-speaking enclaves clinging on at the western edge of an otherwise Anglophone island. Until then, Irish had been something we had to learn at school and struggle through in the evenings with homework, so distant and inconsequential to the reality of growing up in Wicklow. It could have been a different country. For the first time I had a sense of how little I knew of my own homeland.

Today, the town's Gaeltacht identity is its great pride. It's all around you on Spiddal's colourful streets. Bank surrenders its 'k' for a 'c'. Music becomes *ceoil*, food *bia*.

Above it all, the dull grey church rises. As this is summer, teenagers from across Ireland gather in its shadow. I can't help but smile as I weave through them, recognising the ritual from my own days in a summer Irish college. This is where they come to sharpen their language skills and deepen their roots. And the *ceilí*, the traditional Irish set dance, is an intrinsic part of this. It's a rite of passage for many an Irish teen, often the first time they'll be compelled to ask a member of the opposite sex for a dance. A gang of boys approaches, laughter hiding nerves. They steal glances back at the window of a shop, inspecting their hair in their reflections before the machinations commence.

Spiddal is the westernmost outpost of Connemara, the epicentre of traditional Irish culture in Galway. It's a land of rugged mountains and unkempt fields of fern and foxglove, studded with boulders and flecked white with bog cotton. They are ridged by rocky walls that peter out, relics of a bygone age being engulfed by the earth. This is the archetype of postcard Ireland; only Killarney and its neighbouring areas in Kerry come close. Connemara – together with the karst landscape of the Burren in County Clare – is also among the favoured haunts of the cuckoo in Ireland.

Connemara is one of the few places on the Irish mainland where the land seems much as it was centuries ago. With poor soil unsuited to the more robust farming elsewhere, change here has come more slowly. History seems to breathe in Connemara, in a countryside strewn with tombs that date back thousands of years. Perhaps, in a land unchanged, that is why the cuckoo has found Connemara so to its liking.

Its wilder areas are home to the Connemara pony, the only breed of horse native to Ireland. Its lineage is said to descend from the war horses of Celtic times and the steeds of the doomed Spanish armada, who swam ashore to breed with the local horses. A similar story is said of the people of this area. Galway is believed to be the epicentre of the Black Irish, that is, Irish people with uncommonly dark hair and eyes, but with no immediate foreign ancestors to whom these traits can be traced. Legend has it that these Mediterranean features descend from the Spaniards who survived the doom of their fleet, flotsam carried ashore by the Atlantic.

For all its mottled beaches and nascent romances, Spiddal feels like just a meagre outgrowth on the much larger rural splendour that is Connemara. This world opens up to me as I follow the roads deeper into the countryside. It's amazing how fast the bustle of the seaside ebbs away, to be replaced by bucolic silence.

In fact, it's too silent. Bird calls are almost entirely absent, and sightings nearly as scarce. The most vocal are a brood of dunnocks, their cries from deep within a young sycamore summoning their doting parents. As I listen, I wonder if this orchestra of squeals is in fact the solo performance of a cuckoo chick, crying out for food from the bondage of its crumbling nest.

Amid such tranquillity, I think now would be ideal for the male cuckoo to get maximum return from his iconic call. He goes unheard.

In the near total dearth of bird life, the insects predominate. It's like a snapshot from a time long before birds, when insects were the sole commodores of the air. My stroll along the country lanes is harmonised by the incessant clicking of crickets. Dragonflies, in shades of orange and blue, purr past. Ladybirds, like baubles, encumber the leaves of the elms that outflank the roads. They mix and match their carapaces and spots in crimson, orange and yellow, a catalogue of colour. Alighting on a leaf, they wheel in delicate, veined wings beneath their shells before hunting for aphids. And lay your hand on a still rock and, sure enough, ants will flick and twitch its surface into life. Fetid streams tinkle past me as I walk, feeding stagnant pools, air space above them for midges in their hundreds. The pools are buried in little copses of reeds, unhampered by hoe or the farmer's hand.

Completing the profile are the butterflies that flourish in the Irish countryside in summer. Small whites, like animate snowflakes, dance in the breeze. Painted ladies catch the eye with their vivid black-and-orange pallet, ornamented with white spots. Smaller are the meadow browns, an orange flush and eight ball on either wing, all that saves them from a drab brown uniform. They rise and fall along the road's edge, following the contours of the flowers until encountering another of their kind. Then, both spiral upwards in hypnotising combat, spinning away over the fields.

The fields over which they fly nourish no crops, and often are not home even to livestock. Instead, many of them have been allowed to go completely feral.

It makes a nice contrast to the rural scene I'm used to in Wicklow or the midlands, where it often feels like every inch of the countryside has succumbed to ruthlessly efficient agriculture. The fences and walls of these Connemara fields give almost the illusion of human control. Here, random plots are left barren while others hold a handful of cows or donkeys (though, curiously, never sheep), with no apparent strategy for how to maximise any return from them.

The donkeys in particular are synonymous with rural Connemara life. Their faces so often adorn the postcards tourists take home from this corner of Ireland. Nowhere else in the country have I seen them predominate as much as they do here, these creatures that yield no obvious dividend of meat, milk or labour. In the past, they found greater purpose as beasts of burden. They would draw cartloads of turf cut from the bogs or stacks of hay harvested in the fields. But the donkeys, like the farmhands with whom they once worked this land, have been made obsolete by the engine and wheel. They linger on only as an object of affection, a folk memory etched deep in the hive mind of Connemara. They're considered lucky beasts by some. In one garden a grey, woolly male snorts at me as I pass, stamping his feet to intimidate. With no other use about the farm, he has assumed the role of guard dog, sizing up anyone foolish enough to get too close.

June is in its twilight, and determined to depart Connemara with flare. It's fiercely hot, as warm as I can ever remember it being in Ireland. On the country road, the fresh tarmac beneath my feet begins to weep, clinging in strings to my boot heels. With the sea now out of sight, there is no relieving breeze to temper the relentless heat, no clouds above to shield me from the onslaught. It's the kind of weather that wouldn't be out of place on the Mediterranean, the sorts of temperatures that, in another country, might compel you (along with convention) indoors for a siesta. If the Spanish soldiers that supposedly washed ashore in 1588 were to do the same today, they might find the climate quite to their liking.

Boluisce Lake emerges from behind some bushes, a royal blue expanse contouring the outlines of the gentle slopes above it. On a day so hot it's like an oasis in a green desert. It lies at the centre of the landscape, the confluence of roads as well as waters, drawing everything in sight towards it. And as my clothes cling to me and the road ahead starts to dance in the haze, I can think of nothing but the water's cooling caress.

A long path winding through cow fields leads me to the lake shore, sinking abruptly into the water. It's a picture of calm. The sound of the lake lapping against the rocks is salvation from the incessant hum of the crickets. The far shore is treeless for great stretches, as if the lake in its avarice has drained the lifeblood from the soil so that it can sustain nothing but grass. What shrubbery there is, abetted by the tending hand of man, obscures white homesteads like dice tumbled across the landscape. On a day like today, their views must be the envy of every country house in Ireland, taking in not only the lake but the stone-wrapped fields of Connemara. As the afternoon drags on, a haze slithers up through the conifers that vanguard the white wind turbines in the distance. Watching them shimmer, I feel like I've slipped into a fever dream, heat stress getting the better of a dehydrated brain.

My backpack is cool with sweat as I lay it down on the grass, rolling the ache out of my shoulders. Around me, the grass shoots are cooked a golden brown, and even the leaves of the lakeside ferns have begun to peel back to red. Dandelions, though, stand proud with ranks of butter-gold petals peeling back to embrace the sun. In spots, the sunlight is even strong enough to sever the bond between the thin layer of soil and the bedrock beneath; pried free, the peeling earth rises like the bow of a sinking ship, taking its browning carpet of moss with it.

An island punches through the water in the middle of the lake. It's little more than a cluster of rocks, and yet shrubs bristle out from its surface like spines from a hedgehog. Herons overlook the water from within the jumble, concealment the whetstone to sharpen their spear of patience. One lumbers off and low across the lake as I approach, rendered almost black as the backlight mutes its natural silvers.

Though blue from afar, like a mirage the lake reveals its true nature up close. Its water is a rusty brown, heavy with suspension that swirls around smoothed rocks just beneath the surface. I brush my way through briars and rushes that overshadow the shore, checking to make sure no ticks have latched on to exposed calves. This is the domain of the summer insects, and from them I expect no quarter.

Not that birds make no imprint on the shore. A pair of reed buntings has the lake shore to themselves, reaping a rich harvest of the grubs and caterpillars that fester in the undergrowth. The guttural croaks of hooded crows are among the only birdsong that accompanies my path along the lake shore.

But when they desist, amid the radio silence of bird noise, I start to think that the trivialities of life have gotten in the way of this quest. I despair that maybe I have left it too late in the year, that the adult cuckoos have sung themselves out for this summer. Perhaps they are silently stowing away in the undergrowth, biding their time before the long trek back to their wintering grounds in sub-Saharan Africa. Maybe the cuckoos of Connemara have stayed true to the old adage that cuckoos forget their tune in June. With the adults muted, it is the fledgling cuckoos, awkward in the open as they cling to bushes and barbed wire, that I scan for. My eyes and ears strain for meadow pipits, hoping each one will lead to a young cuckoo begging for food.

I didn't fully know what to expect upon returning to Connemara after all these years. My memories of Spiddal and its surrounds had been stretched thin by decades lapsing in between. My route to the shores of Boluisce brought me past the house we'd spent a week in back then. In returning, I'd hoped to find a wilder touch of Connemara, a place abounding in birds, sound-tracked by the call of the cuckoo.

But there is something serene about the embrace of silence, or near-silence, by the lake shore. Silence is a blank canvass for the mind, a space to be populated with your own thoughts and dreams. This is about as quiet as I can recall anywhere being in Ireland. Perhaps, as much as the inspiring view, the dearth of noise is what completes a perfect lakeside artist's retreat. Maybe it's no wonder the Connemara of old spun some of Ireland's most beloved music from its silences, filling this dead space with the beat of the *bodhrán* and the melodious lilt of *sean nós*.

Or perhaps this is all a traveller's folly, an ephemeral island of quiet soon to pass. Isolation, getting the best of me.

July is just a few days away. I leave June, and Connemara, to the donkeys and dancing butterflies.

GREAT SKUA

Inishturk

Once you stray from the well-worn paths, Inishturk offers little easy walking. Far from the gentle, gradual ascent of Tory Island, Inishturk's interior is a rugged range of grassy knolls and ridges. Perplexingly, for an island that looks so small from the sea, and with virtually no trees to smother your view, this terrain can make it difficult to anticipate what lies ahead – and what lies in wait.

Just when you thought you've reached the coast, you summit one slope to find the sea is two or more slopes away. A depression you took at a distance to be a gulley widens out into a rocky ravine. And when peeking over a ridge to see what creatures might lie on the other side, there's no telling what creatures might see *you*.

I spot the skua too late.

One wingbeat and it's aloft, up off its perch on a nearby rock. I turn to make my way back down the slope. But by then there are two skuas, silently closing in. They're twice as big now, having halved the distance between us.

The sheer slope that made the ascent so taxing makes the descent just as awkward. I'm forced to run along its spine rather than down, frantically looking for routes carved by generations of sheep on which I can retreat. Neck tucked into my shoulders, I glance back to see the skuas upon me. It's a shocking role reversal. Most birds flee if you get too close for comfort. Not the skuas. They size up to all comers, as many unfortunate hikers have discovered on remote islands over the years.

Their wings dip at either end as they stoop, webbed feet fully extended as if coming in to land. You would think they'd keep such vulnerable extremities tucked in during an attack, in case their target should have a mind to turn and fight. Not this target. I can think only of the damage that heavy, hooked bill could do to my backpack or jacket – or worse, to my ears or scalp.

They pass one after the other, each less than a metre above my head. Their wingspan is almost as wide as I am tall; seeing so large a bird so close sets my pulse racing. I retreat as fast as I can, but the jagged scree thrown across the sheer grassy face grants me no easy escape. I can't concede to the urge to run even as the skuas show no signs of easing off.

With each stoop, the skuas circle back to gain height. Then they descend on me again, no wingbeats, no croaks, their size and form enough to intimidate. After three warning runs, I put enough distance between us for them to relax and alight again on their ridge, the occasional hoot to remind me of their presence and power. Not wanting to disturb, I give them a wide berth.

The skuas' ridge overlooks a shallow grassy bowl sandwiched between steeper slopes, like a funnel opening into spectacular Atlantic views. In it, three young people – two men and a woman – share a picnic and wine while soaking up the rays. We make small talk as I approach, relishing the seclusion to be found on this oft-overlooked Atlantic isle.

I point out a skua to them, perched ominously on the ridge, looking deceptively small as it watches us from afar. I tell them it's one of the rarest breeding birds in the country.

'Oh, is that the one with the orange beak?' the woman asks.

'No,' I say. 'That's the puffin. That thing eats puffins.'

●●●

Lines of chinstrap penguins meander up and down the volcanic slopes of South Georgia. They make their way to and from nesting scrapes on the high slopes, oscillating between babysitting duty and fishing forays into the Southern Ocean.

Amid the black-and-white mass crawling out of the waves and up the island's slopes is a drop of red. It's a lone penguin, its belly crimson with blood oozing from a wound about its collar. The blood has saturated its plumage, defining every filament on its chest as it labours over boulders and up ash slopes capitulating under its clawed feet. Its attacker was a leopard seal, that great menace of the penguins that populate the Southern Ocean. Now, the penguin, its weakness writ large in leaking blood, faces another peril.

That's when Attenborough's voice kicks in: 'A wounded bird, having escaped almost miraculously from the seal, must now face the merciless skuas.'

Keeping pace with the narration, a brace of huge brown birds dive-bomb into view, tormenting the penguin on its desperate struggle to reach the nest scrape. They circle the colony, picking off chicks and eggs left undefended, hoovering up the offal and detritus left untouched by the penguins. But an injured, exhausted adult also presents a tempting target.

Time and again the skuas swoop, seeming to swallow the penguin in a writhing mass of wings. Their victim opens its gape in protest, screeching at them to retreat. Eventually the skuas alight, perhaps abandoning an aerial assault in favour of hand-to-hand combat on the ground; perhaps biding their time; or perhaps defeated, landing only to rest after a long day surveying the colony. The penguin is last seen slumped forward on the earth, beak dipping slowly, eyes closing in the embrace of exhaustion, and perhaps death. The vignette ends there, the penguin's fate a mystery. The documentary must go on. Other subjects await.

This was my first exposure to the skuas, in a BBC documentary series exploring the wildlife of Antarctica. It was programmes like these that first enamoured me with the work of David Attenborough, and cultivated my love of nature, which I still hold dear.

But perhaps 'merciless' is harsh in this instance. Magnanimity does not factor into the interface between predator and prey. The penguin is trying only to preserve its own life, the skua merely to get a meal. Mercy won't feed the skuas – or their chicks. Whatever the outcome, neither animal is taunting the other. The skua feels no more pleasure in withholding mercy from the penguin than the penguin rejoices in evading the skua. Instead, it is just the primal desires to feed and to survive, those impulses that far precede the nuances applied by man, that fuel the contest between hunter and hunted. It is this that leads to the incremental improvements in form and strategy that divide survival from extinction.

Unlike the penguins, the skuas are not confined to the southern hemisphere. They are just as at home harassing gannets and auks in the North Atlantic as they are menacing penguins in South Georgia. As a group they have a cosmopolitan distribution, though with a bias towards both poles. Europe's western fringe lies towards the southern end of their breeding range.

In shape, the skuas are most like the gulls. They share those long, pointed wings and a head defined by a long, hooked bill. But while the gulls are part-time corsairs, as adept at taking bread intended for ducks as they are harassing smaller birds for food, skuas are professional pirates. They have devoted themselves to a life of pillage on the wing.

They've perfected stealing for survival. Having selected a target – typically an auk with a full crop, or any other bird it can bully – the skua will then dive-bomb it with savage abandon. The attack is so relentless that the victim's desire for relief will very often eclipse the urge to feed its own offspring. If the skua will not relent, and if it can't outpace it in an airborne chase, the target will glibly regurgitate its hard-won catch, surrendering its meal to the skua. While the likes of puffins, guillemots and kittiwakes are the more frequent victims, birds as big as a gannet (a third as big again as the largest skua) are also harassed. Though the razor-sharp bill of the gannet can do damage, if the bird is flying low over the surface of the water, and the incessant bombardment of the skua prevents it from gaining height, there is little it can do to resist. Typically the skua will target the wingtips of the gannet, tipping it off balance and careering it into the water, from whence it cannot get airborne until it surrenders the bootie.

In this way, the skuas are among the few seabirds that don't subsist by fishing for themselves, at least not entirely. And it's not just second-hand fish that piques their appetite. Weak or injured birds – such as penguins maimed by leopard seals – are also taken, as are any eggs left unattended or chicks allowed to stray too far from the nest. Skuas also embrace the role of vultures of the high seas, polishing off the detritus served up by the waves, from carcasses left in the wake of killer whales to waste discarded from trawlers. Such bounties, though, are few and far between, and so an ocean-bound skua will sometimes have to resort to the honest fishing more typical of a seabird, snatching at prey that school just beneath the surface.

There are seven species of skuas terrorising seabirds across the globe. Four of them can be seen off Irish shores, passing to and fro as they rotate between breeding grounds in the Arctic and Scottish Isles and wintering sites further south. But it is the largest of these avian pirates, the great skua, that interests me on this voyage, and draws me to Ireland's western islands in hopes of an audience.

●●●

In wildlife documentaries focussing on seabirds, the skua (if it features at all) is almost invariably the villain, employed to antagonise the more benign auks and kittiwakes on their forays to and from the sea. Rarely, if ever, are the subtleties of skua behaviour explored in any detail.

This is a shame. Far from being mere brutes of the skies, great skuas can apply remarkable cunning to their craft. Different skua populations spread across the North Atlantic have even developed different strategies for different prey. Among the most remarkable are the St. Kilda skuas. This Scottish island hosts huge colonies of Leech's storm petrels. They only return to their nest burrows at night. Ignoring the diurnal instincts of their cousins elsewhere, the great skuas of St. Kilda have tapped into this massive moonlit feast, waiting in the dark to swoop upon the petrels as they come ashore.

Like winged wolves, skuas are also partial to teamwork, pairing up to pin kittiwakes beneath the surface of the water until they drown. Even within a small archipelago like Shetland, regional preferences have arisen, with skuas on some islands picking on kittiwakes while others tend to leave them be.

In Iceland, some great skuas have mastered the art of hunting fulmars and their eggs – no mean feat, given the nauseating face-full that awaits any predator confronted by a vindictive fulmar. The concoction of digested fish and stomach acids is revolting. And before 1940, it was usually enough to deter skuas from predating fulmars. That was the year when skuas hunting fulmars was recorded at an Icelandic fulmar colony for the first time. It has since spread throughout the Icelandic population of great skuas.

Similar specialisations can also be found in how skuas take puffins. While some skuas prefer to attack on the wing, others simply stake out the nesting burrows and engage the puffins on the ground once they return. Elsewhere, some ingenious skuas have learned to circumvent the aerial dive-bombing of Arctic terns by approaching their quarry (the tern chicks) on foot.

In this, is there evidence of a proto-culture? Culture is that which is learned, that which is passed on through the generations, the customs and behaviours that define a population. And in the localised behaviours of disparate great skuas can we see the roots of culture, no less than in the disparate tool-use of chimpanzee troupes or the divergent songs of humpback whales spread across the oceans of the world? It evinces an intelligence in these birds that many people overlook. For the different hunting behaviours favoured by different populations are not purely instinctual. Much as a Patagonian killer whale beaches itself for sea lions only after being shown how by an older relative, the skuas of Iceland only began predating fulmars when they observed that pioneer attempt the audacious catch all those years ago. And the technique spread gradually through the population, a trope that defines this subset of Icelandic skuas from their counterparts elsewhere. In time, will Ireland's burgeoning population of skuas develop feeding behaviours all of their own?

Even if all this is not culture, and amounts only to the predilections of individual skuas, it still speaks to the different personalities to be found across the species – and their supreme adaptability. The disparate foraging techniques favoured by different skuas enables the species to make the most of every resource the North Atlantic and its isles have to offer.

Clearly, there's more to the 'merciless' skuas than mindless butchery.

While many of my targets in this book are in tragic decline, the great skua's arrival as a breeding species is one of Ireland's ornithological success stories of recent times. Previously a passage bird from nesting sites on Orkney and the Hebrides, the skua has gradually expanded its range and was first confirmed breeding in Ireland in 2001. Now small numbers are nesting on the more remote islands off the country's north and west coasts.

Inishturk, off the coast of County Mayo, is among them. Like many islands on the Atlantic fringe, Inishturk was among the areas worst hit by the Great Famine and the subsequent waves of migration that devastated the west coast. In 1841 the island was home to 577 people; by 2016 that number had whittled down to 51. This loss is writ in the ruins strewn across the island. Rock walls border fields no longer farmed. Stone foundations stand for houses and beehive huts long gone. You can see in these traces across the island's interior whisperings of a community once thriving, of untold generations lost to starvation or the call of prosperity across the waves.

Skuas were not the first pirates to make their base here. The old fort at Portdoon, a cove on the island's southern coast, is believed to have been raised by them. They were Danish in origin, and the rocky headlands that coiled around the entrance of Portdoon provided cover for their ships, shielding them from the view of passing vessels until it was too late. This was also where they would come to pool the spoils of their raids, celebrating with a swig of the local tipple, brewed using heather. The recipe for making this legendary beer was lost when the Irish finally retook the island.

If those were the glory days of Ireland's western isles, they have fallen on harder times since. Some, such as nearby Inishark, are now completely abandoned, left to the birds that now flourish in the absence of man.

Inishturk very nearly met the same fate. In 1851, the cruel George Bingham, 3rd Earl of Lucan, evicted the island's entire population – twenty-two families – at gunpoint, shipping them off to workhouses on the mainland.

This fate was meted out to people across Mayo by Bingham, despised as 'The Exterminator' by the native Irish. As the potato crop withered across the west, tenant farmers could no longer meet their rent, and found themselves on the road, bound for the coffin ships or the dreaded workhouses.

Charles Stewart Parnell would later invoke the treatment of the people of Inishturk during the Land War, when he spearheaded the campaign for better rights for tenants and peasant landowners. Bingham saw himself as a visionary, determined to carve a utopian demesne out of his landholdings across Mayo. But his legacy would forever be his horrendous treatment of the people of the county, and of Inishturk in particular, recalled in a stanza of 'The Miscreant of Mayo':

> George Bingham, Earl of Lucan, clearer of the fields,
> Aristocrat of ill renown and curse of those in need,
> the cad that raped all of Mayo, destroyed proud
> Inishturk,
> that paid his devlish henchmen to do his devlish
> work.

In the end, his despotic vision for the island would come to naught. Despite his efforts, the bond between Inishturk and its sons and daughters remained too strong. In the years following the famine, despite the enduring promise of hardship that awaited them, they would trickle back to their island home one by one.

For the longest time, the people of Inishturk endured an insular existence, and visitors from the mainland were rare. Among the most prominent was Robert Lloyd Praeger, esteemed Irish botanist. He spent a week exploring the island with his wife in 1906, as recorded in his classic *The Way That I Went*. Ninety-three years later, legendary kayaker Chris Duff would also stop by the island. His encounters with the old islanders and their traditions are recalled in *On Celtic Tides*, a window into a life now gone:

I looked at his hands, large and weathered with sun spots, fingers that knew the feel of wood. Broad fingernails. In decades past he would have worked on the beach or in a stone shed bending the boards of oak or pine to a plan that existed only in his mind. Each boat different, built to whatever needs the owner had: moving sheep to other islands, fishing for mackerel, or pulling willow lobster traps.

In the dim light of the room, I knew I was looking at a man of the past: the island boat builder. I envied him not only the skill with which he had built those beautiful light craft but also his place in the community. Carpenter and boat builder, there was honour in both titles. I was certain that within [his] memory were stories of island life in the twenties and thirties, stories that he must have heard his parents and neighbours tell around winter fires, memories of storms that must have pounded the seawall and thrown spray onto the panes of the houses above the harbour. Memories of music and laughter, times of plenty and times of need.

Among the vessels that boat builder constructed were almost certainly the local variety of *currach*, the wooden or wicker-framed row boats used along Ireland's west coast for centuries. It's not just skuas that develop different cultural quirks across their various holdings in the North Atlantic. The divergent traditions of Ireland's seafaring communities have their expression in the varying shapes and sizes of *currach* crafted along these coasts. They range from the long, elegant *naomhóg* of Kerry to the compact sea *currach* of Donegal, ideal for navigating rocky inlets to empty lobster pots. Inishturk's *currachs* were usually rowed by three men, and had to be versatile enough to meet the varying demands of island life, from fishing to ferrying residents to the mainland. These days, it's a converted trawler that performs the latter task. Sadly, there are far fewer islanders in need of the services of a *currach* than there used to be.

Though a tragedy for those who once lived here, Inishturk's gradual depopulation has made it an ideal nesting ground for the skua. While fierce enough to defend its nest against almost anything, this bird prefers solitude. An island with few people (and the retinue of nest-raiding pets and rodents that comes with people) is ideal. The other prerequisite is food. Inishturk provides that in the seabirds clawing to cliff-top nests along its edges, ready victims for the skuas to pillage.

While the islanders of yesteryear relied on the sea's bounty or the sheep that grazed the island's slopes for their income, these days Inishturk's stock in trade is tourism. Visitors flock here to enjoy the Atlantic views to be had along its well-worn hiking routes. But finding a skua will require a detour. I follow the stony path as far as the island's only lake, in the shadow of Mount Common. Here, the grass that predominates elsewhere cannot venture, and the rushes grow tall. In unison they bend over in the breeze, the anaemic fins of so many sharks. The water, royal blue from any distance, is choking with pondweed beneath the surface. A female mallard makes an island of herself at the lake's centre, circled by three ducklings, fighting their way through the submerged tendrils.

Striking off for the heart of the island, the ground is soft and crunchy underfoot. Here, off the walking routes that loop through the island, solitude reigns. When planning my trip to Inishturk, I wondered if, like Tory, it might make a suitable summer residence for corncrakes. But away from the coast, I can scarcely see the beds of nettles male corncrakes need to call from. Not even the rabbits seem to have reached here. Instead, it's a sea of grass, almost shorn down to the ground by the sheep that have much of the island to themselves. Their ears are pierced through with yellow tags, their coats blotched with red and green, a painless branding. They stand sentry atop every ridge and outcrop I pass, heads raised to stare me down with curved horns.

The other plants here are pariahs, specks of colour in an expanse of grass and bleached stone. A lone thistle stands by the hiking trail, fighting the pull of the Atlantic wind as best it can. Strands of bog cotton cling together as if for strength, their filaments strung out by the breeze. Prettier is the occasional bird's-foot trefoil, its flower like golden coffee beans.

After a struggle through the interior of the island I reach the coast. Gulls float incessantly overhead, as if trying to keep the whole island under constant surveillance. They cast skua-shaped shadows across the ground as they do so, white underwings blackened by the overhead sun when I look up; a micro-disappointment each time.

The cliffs echo to the barks of fulmars, circling about like flies over a summer pond. Out on the water, a floating mass of auks rises and falls with the swell, content to let the ocean massage their stomachs as the sun teases the wet from their wings. Any thought of getting close to the cliff is killed by a sudden gush of wind, like an airstrike in the dead of night. Were this to catch me too close to the edge, I'd surely lose my footing.

Instead, I try to follow the contours of the island south. It's as if Inishturk, in a bid to hide itself in some winter storm, has mimicked the undulation of the sea; a snapshot of a storm impressed on earth and rock.

My travails are to the piping of ringed plovers. Like the skuas, they nest on the ground. But while the skuas can rely on bulk and outrage to keep their chicks safe, the diminutive plovers must take a different tack. As a plover loops around me, it sweeps the ground with its primaries, feigning injury, a decoy to lure me away from the nest.

Then, up ahead, a skua emerges out of the ether. It's some distance away yet, but there's no doubt in my mind. This is no juvenile gull, deceiving me with mottled greys. All about, its feathers are the uniform brown of the skua, broken only by white patches on the wings. These are cut clear as it banks over a ridge. The sunlight seems to refract through them, the way it might crawl through the stained windows of an old glasshouse.

It's not alone. There are three skuas, rising and falling above the slopes. Even in their dealings with each other, their aggressive nature shines through. Two of them seem to chase each other. Powerful wingbeats give devastating speed to such a large bird. When one concedes the chase and goes to ground, it assumes the classic skua pose: wings thrown back, chest bulging out and head raised with its beak agape. It's like it wants to squeeze every square inch of size out of its form, wings beating as if to rouse the very wind into battle. Even though its pursuer now circles unchallenged, it insists on claiming the same stretch of ridge. And so the two skuas are perched beside each other, honking until their wings fold and their grievance is forgotten.

Perhaps this deceptively aggressive interaction is a sign of visceral affection. For as well as being cunning killers, skuas are also devoted partners and parents. Not for them are the ephemeral liaisons between corncrakes on isles to the north of here. Skuas pair for life. Maybe by this energetic display, this mated pair reaffirm their bond. It could be a test of strength, making sure they each have the vigour to pursue seabirds into submission for as long as it takes to fledge their chicks.

They stand in the open, relaxed now, surveying their island domain. A peace descends as I watch them. The skuas rise again, and float off out of sight, vanishing behind the ridge on which they perched.

Foolishly, not knowing how close it would bring me to their nest, I follow them.

●●●

Coming here, a view of a distant skua was all I had hoped for. Still establishing themselves on the west coast, the embryonic population of skuas can do without disturbance. I'm regretful that the birds I encountered wasted any energy seeing me off, and so give them a wide berth.

I make my way back to the one village on the island, a smattering of houses flowing from the main port. The route takes me back past relics of an island once flourishing, those walls and husks of houses, homes for farmers long passed. Looking out to the horizon, the islands and peninsulas of Mayo seem to hold Inishturk in their embrace. At the heart of it all, Croagh Patrick commands the skyline, rising like an arrowhead in the distance.

Out of nowhere, a skua powers past. A near-panic sets in. Surely I have not crossed another nest?

My eyes follow the skua into the distance. As it begins to wheel I prepare to break out in a jog, expecting it to descend on me with venom. It doesn't. It seems almost to freeze in mid-air, a flag flying proud over the heart of Inishturk. Then it completes its circuit, succumbing to the sea breeze that carries it away over the island.

RING OUZEL

Gap of Dunloe

Thrush is not the first bird to come to mind when you think high, wild mountains. Surely this is the domain of eagles, falcons and ravens; creatures befitting this vast towering landscape. It's hardly a place for garden birds, habituated to the shadow of man.

Only, the ring ouzel is no garden bird. Where the blackbird is happy to reside in suburbia, the ouzel has not shaken its preference for wild places, rocky promontories where disturbance is hard to come by. Our other thrushes might thrive in lowland glades, dragging worms from the wet earth or chipping away at autumn apples. Not the ring ouzel. It's the only summer thrush we have in Ireland, and spends most of that window (April to September) in the remotest corners of our highest mountain peaks.

The ring ouzel is one of six thrushes that divide Ireland between them at different times of year. It's the only one that migrates to Ireland to breed, with two (the redwing and fieldfare) joining us for the winter, complementing the blackbirds, song thrushes and mistle thrushes that live here year-round.

In form and colour, the ring ouzel is most like the blackbird. It is this similarity that probably sees many ouzels dismissed as blackbirds by mountaineers, catching a glimpse of a fleeing black streak as it dashes away among the boulders. But with good views the distinction is clear. True, they share the black-brown colour dynamic that splits the genders among blackbirds. But the breast of the ring ouzel is much scalier than on a blackbird, the feathers etched in silver like a hundred overlapping arrowheads. And in the males, the separation is carved in a white crescent, like a quarter-moon, a standard splashed across his chest. The crescent can also be seen in the female ouzel, but is more muddied, as if the browns of her head and neck have seeped into it.

Summering ouzels are confined solely to our highest peaks. Here, they have a fief all to their own, largely free from the competition of their lowland-dwelling cousins. The ouzel further avoids any conflict by vacating Ireland entirely during winter. This is when our shores become a refuge for thrushes (including more blackbirds) from the continent – thrushes that might have an eye for the same shrinking supply of food.

It is to the mountains of Kerry that I have come to find my ring ouzel, to the famed Gap of Dunloe, a glacial pass that divides the MacGillicuddy's Reeks from the Purple Mountains. I've heard that birds can be heard singing on the slopes above the gap. In some years, more intrepid males will even call from near the little bridges that arch over its floor. With July well underway, it's possible if not likely I've left it too late to hear one. But stranger things have happened.

Never a common bird here to begin with, the ring ouzel has been in sharp decline across Ireland for decades. In 1900 it bred in twenty-one Irish counties. Now it's confined to Donegal and Kerry. Pioneering birds might venture beyond these polar outposts at either end of the country, evading surveyors in mountain passes and the lofty ridges. But it's still been a staggering shrinkage in the species' breeding range over such a short period of time.

What's more worrying is that the exact causes of this are not fully understood. While the upland habitat it prefers has come under pressure over the past century (less heather, more hikers and grazers) this onslaught alone is not enough to explain the drastic drop in visiting ouzels. Perhaps the root of this decline lies in its wintering grounds in Spain and North Africa. Here, it relies on juniper berries for its winter crop after gorging on earthworms and insects during the Irish summer. (The bond is so strong that the ouzel's winter distribution is believed to be controlled mostly by juniper; it is the yuletide sustenance for the ouzel while its temperate cousins devour hawthorn and holly berries.) Or maybe its plight is linked to broader environmental and climactic factors, the scale and implications of which we are yet to fully grasp.

●●●

Though striking enough to stir the imagination, the sights and smells about the gap of Dunloe are more than enough to keep you grounded. All along the valley, the road is blobbed with horse dung, the hallmark of the jaunting cars that traverse the gap for a living. But even this execrable resource does not go to waste here. Chaffinches scavenge from it, rooting around for the softened pips and kernels, letting the formidable digestive tract of the horse do the hard labour.

My first steps on the road into the gap are in dismay. I find myself immersed in forest. Holly trees with syringed leaves arch over mossy boulders by the roadside. I have an endearing passion for such countryside. It might be perfect for blackbirds, but this is no home for ring ouzels. Pressing on, at first you only get glimpses of mountains through the trees, teases of the kind of terrain the ouzels might call their summer home. They contrast the two divergent realms in which the thrushes of Ireland build their nests.

Soon though, you are in the gap proper. The trees concede, surrendering the floor of the great valley to a sea of ferns and beach saplings, feeding into steep slopes on either side. Ahead they rise, one after the other as if in bravado, challenging each other to scrape the sky with their magnitude. On this overcast July day some succeed, their peaks obscured by wisps of cloud.

All about me, the wind makes for a constant rustle among the leaves. It whirls about in frenetic indecision, unsure which route to pursue through the gap. It also makes a mess out of the stringy coats of the sheep that graze here, their yellow horns growing in scalloped layers like the mountains on which they feed. They are as integral a part of the furniture of the gap as the piebald horse and jaunting car. I even see them lounging in pairs in front gardens, bellies bulging, mistaking them at first for oversized, shaggy dogs.

The floor of the gap is pockmarked with five little lakes, the lifeblood of the valley. The first, Coosaun Lough, is hemmed in by rushes and pond plants that festoon the shoreline. Like all the lakes it's fed by the River Loe, struggling through a phalanx of boulders. As I circle around it a female blackbird swoops across its surface to her nest deep in the bushes: a test, a reminder to me to remain focussed. The larger Black Lake soon follows. Its waters are greyed by the clouds above, churning like an ocean storm, a microcosm of chaos at the heart of an otherwise serene valley. The only peace on its surface can be seen in the green pond leaves, like a bed of open mussels guarding the shoreline.

All life in the gap seems to flow out from the lakes; existence gets more precarious the more it strays from the water's edge. Ferns and gorse bushes grab a foothold where they can on the lower slopes. Some of the bushes have surrendered their leaves, thorns and flowers to the wind, with dead twisted branches their only legacy, islands of decay in an ocean of green. The dandelions that seem to crawl across the valley floor add licks of yellow. They remain tiny, as if terrified to grow so tall as to challenge the supremacy of the Reeks looming overhead.

Although the plants make their mark, at its heart the gap is a place of stone. The lower slopes are strewn with boulders. They are the excrement of the glaciers that carved out this narrow pass millennia ago. Further up, the rock peels back like the layers of a split onion. The hardened path that you follow through the gap makes a tightened snare for the percussion of horseshoes. The valley rumbles to the sound of the clop of hooves on stone as they come thundering past, jaunting car heaving with tourists. They quicken and slacken with the ebb and flow of the valley floor, a drummer building to a crescendo before fading to a finish. Their noise is superseded by the distant shouts of tourists seesawing through the valley. They test how much echo they can yield from its slopes, amplifying the enormity of the space around them.

Tourism has a history here. Although Kerry was a theatre for much brutal action during the War of Independence, before that it was an English monarch who helped reverse the fortunes of the impoverished Gap of Dunloe. Queen Victoria enjoyed a pony ride through the gap in the 1860s, retinue in tow, one of the very first tourists to do so. News of its beauty soon spread in the media storm that engulfed the Queen's visit. Before long, the gap became the fashionable montane retreat. Visitors from across Ireland and Britain arrived to marvel at the works sculpted by glaciers long withered to water.

The gap lends itself easily to romance. Bartholomew Colles Watkins, among the foremost of Ireland's nineteenth-century landscapists, was enamoured with its misty eloquence. Looking at his work now, the paths through the valley are much as they were then, with sheep trailing through just as they do today, speaking to the timelessness harboured here. Indeed, the beauty and tranquillity of this region would prove fatal to Watkins; it was in Kerry that he caught the illness from which he never recovered.

Mountains might make for wonders on canvas, but they also provide a formidable natural defence. It was this strategic import that made this region an ideal base for Norman adventurers. They would go on to fortify the castle at Dunloe, employing their craft of castle-making to create a base capable of withstanding Gaelic onslaught. Generations later, the forces of Oliver Cromwell would also visit the gap as they cut a bloody path through the Irish countryside.

What followed were decades of hardship for the rural Catholics of Kerry, burdened by the Penal Laws. Their salvation came in the form of Donal Caoch, a champion of the oppressed Catholics who flocked to sanctuary on his lands. From their ranks he would raise his own private militia with which to harass the surrounding Protestant landowners. The Gap of Dunloe was used to funnel cattle stolen during his raids.

Nearly two hundred years later, in 1920, the castle at Dunloe would come under the ownership of Howard S. Harrington, a wealthy American, who reprised the tradition of the Gaelic lords of yore by declaring himself a chieftain.

His main contribution to the demesne and its surrounding valley was the plants he imported from around the world to augment his estate. Maybe, had juniper been among them, he could have tempted migrating ouzels to stay just a while longer.

●●●

As you follow the only road through the gap, the valley gets narrower and narrower. Two slopes rise in sheer splendour on either side, like the pillars of a great gate welcoming you into the realm of the ring ouzel; a diminutive lord for such a mighty castle. A ceremonial line of sycamore and spruce guards the way. They loom over an abandoned stone house with ply-board windows and a rusted roof. Other traces of man linger here too, long after their utility has been exhausted. Stone walls incur as far as the scree and steep ascent will permit; a doomed attempt to stake a flag to the gap and reclaim it from the forces of nature.

It is in this wilder space that I start to sink into the sounds of birds once more. I hear distant piping and clicking – maybe ring ouzel, maybe not. I follow a black dash through the bushes until it reveals itself to be a male blackbird, standing proud on a mossy rock, framed in little ferns. A branch beside an abandoned house makes an ideal perch for a spotted flycatcher, muted silver in the grey light. Like the ouzel it's a summer visitor, here to raise its young on the invertebrate bounty before retreating to warmer climes to overwinter. He darts back and forth about the undergrowth, rhythmically returning to his favourite post, a base from which to launch more forays for food. While he worries the flies in the bushes that mushroom around the dead homestead, a grey wagtail polishes off little things that creep on the lake shore. He rises, long tail seeming to drag in the air, to perch on a rock, an attractive coupling of yellow and grey, before being startled back to the lakeside by an approaching horse and car.

With the sheer faces of the Purple Mountains and MacGillycuddy's Reeks rising on either side of you, you feel as if you're entering a great stadium, the terraces dizzyingly steep to afford avian spectators a view of the drama below. To my right the peaks of the Reeks are jagged, as if someone has taken a bite out of them. With no other release, the wind channels through the valley, sending rhythmic waves through the grass where it finds purchase on the slopes.

Ferns and tufts of laurel spread out among the boulders. The latter is an invasive species staking a claim to the gap with shiny, cyanide-laced leaves. Prettier is the heather; here and there, the rocks are crusted with its purple blooms. Closer to the path, the colour comes from the fuchsia bushes, an invader straight from the South African veldt, with round-tipped tendrils hanging from violet bells and dark berries cocooned on their branches. Perhaps they descend from those exotic plants brought here by Howard S. Harrington all those years ago. Willow warblers spin between them, beaks full of food for their nestlings. On the other side of the road, tiny white blossoms spring from the mud of the last of the lakes pooled at the bottom of the gap.

Further up, green gashes crisscross the Purple Mountain like scar tissue. From on high, all I can hear are the plaintive bleats of sheep, as if calling for help from deep within the purgatory of the mountain. I approach a bridge, one of several that traverse the gap. A panicked trilling rings out, a machine gun of tweets. Like a blackbird. Maybe a blackbird. But for a moment I think maybe an ouzel, startled by my approach.

I look for a bird standing proudly atop a branch or rock. This would be the male ring ouzel, no longer furtive but keen to express his vocal prowess, and be seen to be doing so. It is with this song that he would declare dominion over this stretch of slope. And only in the open can he employ the visual panache of his white chest crescent to impress the females. Perhaps, like the red combs of the male grouse that share the high slopes, it is with this that he visualises his fitness and genetic vigour. Unlike his blackbird counterpart, the male ring ouzel has no golden beak with which to draw the eye. His bill is tempered with black, its yellows watered down as if it were dipped in ink. It is with the crescent that he must impress. And on a mountain slope where no white can be seen save the wool of sheep, I'm hoping it will stand out.

I scan the slopes, a magnet for movement among the rocks and greenery. But the call's maker is at one with the scree, perhaps knowing better than to draw attention by making for the higher ground. If there are ouzels here, they are hiding with a precision that eclipses their bold markings. The black male matches the shadows that lurk between the boulders. The brown female vanishes into the heather, at one with the very roots of the mountain itself.

A performance starts, a desolate *obbligato* from up on high. It's clearly a thrush, the whistles and clicks cut through with short pauses. It flows from an unknown spring on the slopes, this hesitant birdsong buried in the breeze. It feels like a whispering between the mountains, like the delusions that haunt wayward wanderers lost on a mountain road. All the other birds of the valley – the pipits, the chaffinches, the linnets – are silent now. I enjoy a private audience, as an unseen tenor waxes in obscurity to an empty theatre. To my shame, I'm at a loss to discern if this is the lilting song of the ring ouzel or the more melodious tune of the blackbird, straining to discern the emotional content of the performance. The ping of a cyclist's bell snaps me out of my trance. The singing stops, abandoning the terraces to the wind. Frustrated, I push deeper into the gap.

Once you work your way through the bottleneck between the mountains, the valley floor widens before you. There is space again, space for a kind of wild pasture to flourish and for sheep to keep it in check, following the progress of the road. Thistles emerge, and a siskin makes short work of their seeds, discarding the white effluent to give form to the breeze.

Looking back, the slopes of the Purple Mountain and the Reeks don't seem so divided. Instead, they cross like the knuckles of two fists slotted into one another. Between them, in a v, the fields of Kerry spread out in the distance; the home of song and mistle thrushes and other farmland birds, far below the demesne of the ring ouzel. From up on high the ouzel must command an even more glorious view of the Kerry countryside, perhaps as far as the distant Atlantic beyond.

Heading on, the road zig zags up to an overlook. At the top, it stands at the precipice of a vast bowl, a carpet of mixed conifer and broad-leaved forest at its heart, ridged by hills all around: the Black Valley.

It's a far cry from the barren gap that guards it. Though still tinged by the mountains' roughness, there is more pasture here, easier grazing for the sheep than scraping a living off rocks in the gap. While their counterparts on the high slopes have grown shaggy, the sheep here are sheered bald, their red markings fading to pink the way strawberry syrup bleeds into ice-cream. Below, a few houses dot the valley floor, white and yellow lice grown fat in a green pelt. As if to complete the idyllic picture, a church bell welcomes midday as it echoes through the valley. Ignore the telegraph poles strung about the fields and you could be in a scene from centuries past.

Indeed, this valley was the last place in the entire country to acquire telegraph poles. The Black Valley was the final holdout in Ireland to join the national grid, in 1976. Until then, it was almost a hidden kingdom, a parallel realm wrapped up and shielded by the mountains. A local joke goes that the valley's name stems from the lack of lamplight that left it in darkness for so long. I'd prefer to believe that it has a less prosaic origin, steeped in a time when local factions contested ownership of the valley. If such a title was earned in the past, it has long since been outgrown. Taking in the view, the valley is anything but black.

Somewhere off to the west lies Carrauntoohil, the highest peak in the country. I've read that ring ouzels nest on its upper slopes. What an adventure that would be: ascending Ireland's highest mountain in search of one of its rarest birds. A quest to remember – but one for a summer yet to come.

I round a corner to find the queen of the valley, surveying her domain from a roadside perch. Not an ouzel, or raven, but a peregrine. I'm aghast to find myself so close to such an awesome predator. It's a bird that's captivated me ever since I saw one stoop at full speed over Wicklow Head as a boy – and one I've not seen since.

At such close range her size impresses – I judge her to be female, based on bulk alone. She's barely ten metres above the trail, holding on with huge yellow feet. She studies me through obsidian eyes as I walk past, head twitching to take me in from every angle. She's still enough to allow me to return the gesture, taking in every detail of her heavy, hooked bill, moustachial stripes and barred chest. She's like an exhibit stolen from a museum, perched proud atop a bed of heather and withering mountain soil. As I edge closer, I see what has her glued to this spot: an explosion of feathers on the grass. Nearby, a hooded crow on the deck, legs frozen, struck from the air by a feathered bullet. The peregrine is so prominent it's like she's taking pride in her work, keen for passers-by to admire her perfect strike. But more likely, she's just found the crow (almost her equal in size) too heavy to carry aloft. And so she retreats to higher ground, safe to watch me and the tourists pass before descending to feed.

In peak tourist season her patience is tested. A procession of jaunting cars and vehicles passes by, the automobiles slowed behind the trotting horses, all of their passengers passing under the peregrine's gaze. None of them notice her, high on her rock, regarding them with a benign curiosity. Eventually she takes off, doing a lap of the mountainside, stretching the wings before resuming her vigil. As I make my way back up towards the lip of the valley, I look back to appreciate her once more, framed against the Reeks that tower in the background like the green folds of a great curtain. A picture of Ireland's wild mountains, as they were for centuries – and as they are once again.

Peregrines were once in sharp decline across Ireland. The pesticides that infested their food congealed deep within the females. Insidious, these softened the shells of their eggs so much they would fissure under the weight of the incubating adults.

Now, even in the most conservative corners of rural Ireland, pesticide use is waning. More and more people are awake to the damage it causes, especially to our top predators. And with pesticides in retreat, the peregrines have begun to rise again. They no longer rank among our most endangered birds. It's been a remarkable recovery, and a sign of how man and bird can coexist. Seeing her here gives me hope that these surrounds can offer shelter to creatures not so fortunate, creatures whose fate remains uncertain. Creatures like that elusive ring ouzel.

The gap is no less scenic as I embark on the long road back to Kate Kearney's Cottage, the inn that marks its entrance. The wind that defused as I entered the Black Valley regains its vigour and purpose in the gap, funnelled forever through the Purple Mountain and the Reeks. It sets the long grass on the Reeks dancing, gleeful that it remains uncropped by the sheep patrolling the road.

Walking through the gap, I hear it again, the blackbird-like song. It's a whispering on the wind, like a memory of the mountain, emanating from the slopes. A sorrowful reprise to farewell tired travellers. I study the Reeks for a moment, but not for too long. The singer desists. Around me, the stadium feels empty.

Then, from the other side, a horrendous squealing. Far above, tearing across the slopes, are two peregrines. A male and female, made obvious by the gulf in size; the female looks easily twice the size of her mate. Perhaps this is the same female I saw in the Black Valley, choosing to hunt there but make her nest on the inaccessible slopes above the Gap of Dunloe.

They circle about as if trapped in each other's orbit before locking talons, perhaps in a food exchange, and wheeling. The female swings her shrill mate in loops. He flaps frantically, forgetting his aerial prowess in her embrace, almost comical in his inelegance. When they part, his wings beat to cushion his fall, graceless, tail fanned as he claws at the rocky slope.

BARN OWL

Maynooth

Behind me, the noises of the night begin to bleed away. Past a certain point on the way home, the sounds of nightclub music and drunken laughter can no longer make traction on my ears. I'm on the last stretch now, guided by the lamplight that casts crescents over the grey footpath. The occasional car outraces me. Sometimes I pass a couple ambling the other way. But mostly I'm alone. The wee hours march on. My hunger is satisfied. Bed beckons.

Before I can embrace the duvet, there's a hill to overcome. Cul-de-sacs peel off on either side of the road carved into it, trees looming beside them. The lights are out in most of the houses, the curtains drawn. The streetlamps are more spread out now, and the moon behind me renders little light from the dark sky.

It's the movement that catches me as much as anything. Looking up, about halfway up the hill, a pale shape like an apparition bounces above the trees on long, rounded wings. I gasp I'm so taken aback. I've made this walk too many times to recall, and never had an encounter like this. But it's fleeting, as the mystery creature floats silently away over the houses and quiet gardens.

●●●

I knew I'd just seen my first wild owl. In Ireland we're lucky enough to have three. The short-eared defies the nocturnal habits owls are famous for, haunting our wetlands during the winter by day. Its cousin, the long-eared owl, holds fast to the traditions of the family, patrolling the woodlands of Ireland by dark. Logic would dictate that this was the bird I saw. It's the most common owl we have, and the hill on which my house sits overlooks the kind of forest perfect for long-eared owls. And though its mottled brown plumage helps keep it concealed by day, this camouflage itself hides the paler underparts of the owl, unsheathed only in flight.

But if there's one enduring memory from that night, one thing that holds fast through the tiredness and fumbled attempts at reconstructed memories, it's the paleness. For sure, long-eared owls are pale below. But this, as I recall, was a ghastly white, more reminiscent of the other native owl we have.

Few birds have staked a claim to the Irish psyche more than the barn owl. Ask any Irish person to name one owl species, they'd almost certainly say barn. Ask any Irish child to draw you an owl and the white-fronted creature that results will most closely match the profile of a barn.

Like a spectre haunting the countryside, it's a bird steeped in myth. Its rasping shriek, far from the classic hoot attributed to owls on the silver screen, is a siren straight from the underworld. It would earn the bird a sinister association with death. In Ireland, the barn owl's cry is thought to have inspired the *banshee*, parting her hair with a cursed comb, wailing when a family member was about to pass. Its status as an emissary to the doomed was strengthened by its habit of haunting graveyards. By night, it formed a pasty, ethereal lure that tempted drunkards to their grave on their way home. Or, perhaps, cemeteries just made for good hunting.

By day, the owl is in absentia, hidden away in the hollowed recesses of a tree trunk or amid the lofts of a barn. It alone assumes avian predatory duties on the farm (or above the graveyard) by night; a silent torment to rodents and shrews when the kestrels, kites and harriers have all been defeated by the setting sun. From an aesthetics point of view, the owl's aversion to daylight is unfortunate, robbing observers of the chance to appreciate its stunning feathering: the face and chest pure white, shading into a fawn saddle. Erupting from the face, the eyes tempered by the night, dipped in the darkness for which they have evolved. The back and upper wings are streaked through with electric blue, like raindrops, bordered in black. It's like a winter rain, the owl's great nemesis, has left a permanent imprint on its plumage, a striking reminder of its frailty, shaming it into hiding whenever the clouds burst.

The barn owl's striking plumage also makes it even more dependent on man-made cover; unlike the long-eared owl, it can't rely on cryptic camouflage to conceal it during the day, hence the need to stowaway in barns.

Hunting at night requires a specific kit. Most birds of prey kill by sight, but not the barn owl. Its hearing is among the most acute in the entire avian pantheon. It has to be. Hunting mice by day is difficult enough. But in the dark, when they're invisible amid the shoots of long grass, sound is by far the better option. Like the directional forked tongue of a snake, the owl is able to use the minute differences in sound received by either ear to steer the way as it flies in near-total darkness over the fields. It is aided by asymmetry in its ears: the right ear points slightly upwards, while the left faces the ground. This gives it an advantage when pinpointing sounds both across the azimuth (horizontal) and elevation (vertical). And it's critical. A fox or a cat need only hear the mouse on the horizontal plane. The barn owl also has to angle its strike from above.

That benign, heart-shaped face plays a pivotal role in this sophisticated navigation setup. The broad facial ruff, like a satellite dish, is sculpted perfectly to steer sounds into the ears, hoovering up any rustles as the owl covers tremendous ground with each hunt (more than any other nocturnal bird). Even the feathers themselves are particularly fine, a perfect backdrop to amplify the acoustics of rodents tunnelling through grass. All of this combines to devastating effect; barn owls can home in prey in total darkness.

Of course, all of this precision amounts to naught if the victim hears you first. The barn owl has evolved to make sure it goes unheard on its night-time forays across the farm. Everything, from the elliptical shape of its wings to the distribution of its bodyweight, is designed to get maximum movement with minimal sound. Serrations on the leading edge of the wings complement the velvety soft feathers on top, controlling the airflow and keeping friction to a minimum. By the time the victim hears the owl plunging on top of it, it's too late.

Broad wings also allow for a slow, controlled approach, pinpointed for the kill. Cruising over the farm, the owl only speeds up to attack mode once the target has been acquired. Then, it dives, talons spread and head pulled back, eyes shut just in case. Very often the target is not killed by the initial strike, and so a nip to the back of the neck is needed to finish the job. Even if the owl's coordinates are wrong and it misses entirely, all is not lost. The grounded owl will stand motionless, waiting for the target's movement to betray its location.

Between them, the brown rat, two species of mouse and one species of vole make up the bulk of the barn owl's diet in Ireland. Voles are relatively rare here; the field vole, the barn owl's main prey in Britain, is altogether absent from Ireland. Because of this, our barn owls are more likely to take rats and mice than their counterparts across the Irish Sea.

As such, you'd think the barn owl would be a cherished addition to the menagerie of birds living on the farm. Each brood of chicks gobbles through an immense number of rodents (a family can eat nearly four thousand in a single year). This decimates the number of pests farmers have to contend with. And yet the barn owl has been a species in decline for some time. This has been much publicised; I can think of few other Irish birds whose plight has elicited more attention.

Its shrinking numbers have robbed rural Ireland of one of its most charismatic denizens. Just as modernisation has largely put paid to the old myths that the barn owl helped spawn, it has also wrought its toll on the owl itself. Efficient farming leaves no space for abandoned outhouses and underused barns, the kinds of spaces that made ideal nesting spots for generations of owls.

This alone cannot explain the decline; barn owls were nesting in tree holes for millennia before they took to barns. Other factors have also come into play. Grass shorn to the scalp has deprived the owl of the rough pasture it likes to hunt in. Road networks winding through the countryside proved a siren to the barn owl, embracing the bird in a double envelopment. Roads chewed up more and more of the countryside the owl needed to hunt in. But, perversely, roadside verges also made for ideal hunting trails – at a grave cost. Prowling low over the ground, late at night, the owl is vulnerable to collisions. Blinded by headlights, and slow-moving by nature, it cannot evade oncoming traffic in time. It's tragic that the only barn owl many people will see in the flesh is so often strewn beside a motorway.

Even the very rodents the owls depend upon are now, so often, severely tainted, vectors for rodenticides that leak into the wider ecosystem. Predators, like the barn owl, suffer the end result. Mouse by poisoned mouse, they ingest more and more of the insidious poison until they are finally overcome. What's worse, these toxins can be hereditary, sullying the next generation of owls.

The climate also doesn't help. The soft, silent feathers of the barn owl lack the robustness needed to shake off heavy rain. The owl needs dry conditions in which to hunt – conditions that are far from certain, even at the zenith of an Irish summer. A cold, wet winter can mean many lean nights for the owls, roost-bound, tormented by prey scurrying about beyond their grasp. Just a few centimetres of snow can be fatal, creating a blanket that shields their prey from surveillance. Small wonder, then, that the highest rate of mortality occurs between December and March.

It is this aversion to adverse weather that makes the barn owl an anomaly in Ireland. True, it ranges further than any other owl, breeding on every continent except Antarctica. But it's most at home in warm, dry climates: the African savannah, the Mediterranean scrub, the Australian bush. Its path into northern Europe was paved by the spread of farming, terraforming the landscape, and the proliferation of prey that came with it. Now, that same food source is being jeopardised. In Ireland, the relative shortage of small mammal species robs the owl of alternative foods to tap into should the mice, rats or shrews also have a bad winter.

The net result of all this has been a more than 50 per cent drop in barn owl numbers in Ireland since the 1970s. This has spurred a concentrated response to save the species. Nesting boxes have been installed across the countryside to compensate for the loss of old buildings. Pesticides, the great bane of all birds of prey, are being discouraged. The benefits of owls about the farm are proselytised more than ever.

Whether all this will be enough to save Ireland's barn owls remains to be seen. But it's surely a good start.

•••

Returning to Maynooth after an absence of years brings a buzz with it, like that feeling you get when about to see a long-lost friend. This is where I went to university, and so is tied to a flurry of good memories. They are brought back to life as I stroll the gridded streets and leafy south campus of the university. I try to recall everything as it was, noticing subtle changes in the structure, the natural wastage of shops and restaurants that occurs over time, the occasional lick of new paint.

Maynooth markets itself as Ireland's university town, with a strong pedigree as a centre of learning. For a time it housed the largest seminary in the world, and still has a strong bond with the church; older relatives, hearing I was studying in Maynooth, were convinced I was bound for the priesthood. Because of the university, it feels like the natural rhythm of Maynooth runs counter to most Irish towns I've known. During term there's a buzz and energy about the place. But now, in late summer, things are more sedate.

If barn owls form a conduit to an Ireland long gone, then they are well placed in Maynooth. It was here, in the fertile lowlands of north Kildare, that the FitzGeralds, among the foremost Anglo-Norman families to accompany Strongbow on his conquest of Ireland, would be rewarded for their service with land and titles. And it was here that they would cultivate one of the greatest dynasties ever seen in Ireland, playing an integral role in regional power structures for centuries to follow. Such was their influence that they even made Maynooth the capital of Ireland – if only for a short while. They cemented their hold on the region in typical Norman fashion: a castle, the ruins of which still guard the entrance to the south campus.

Later, when they had firmly embedded themselves in the fabric of north Kildare, and the moat and imposing walls were no longer needed, they fashioned a new home for themselves: Carton House. While the castle was concerned with the utility of holding and controlling a hostile territory, the house was (and remains) a symbol of the dynasty's lasting opulence. It's a lavish, sprawling estate, holding sway over hundreds of acres of the surrounding countryside.

It is here that I have decided to chance my arm looking for barn owls.

●●●

Above the estate, the August sun is sullied by clouds, closing in about it like a curtain. It strangles what wisps of sunlight linger on the horizon, like gold smeared over with polish. The sky between the clouds is still bright, but little of its glow reaches the ground. With the brightness goes the saturation, and everything appears dull. The incessant breeze is a relief from the heat of the dying daylight. Now and then, a speck of rain cools my forehead. Given my quarry, I hope it holds off.

This is birding by moonlight. It's an altogether different experience from what I'm accustomed to. Most of my birdwatching takes place in the early morning. This is when most birds are most active, when they get a flurry of foraging complete and the generous light makes for easy viewing.

The character of the evening is wholly different. There's a lethargy in the birdlife about the estate, the energy of a long day sapped from them. Three mute swans, parents and a grown cygnet, let the current of the river carry them along. Even the lively house martins, swooping above its water, have begun to decorate the bare branches of a dead tree, ephemeral substitutes for shoots. The tiredness in the air is one I can relate to. I'm not used to searching for birds this late, with a full day's travel behind me. If there are barn owls here, they'll have the advantage of a long rest. I hope my senses, dulling with the onset of dusk, don't let me down.

Spread out before me, the landscape is a patchwork of grassy spaces and trees. Most of the grass is cut into a golf course. But, to my delight, there is still longer, uncut grass where rodents can hide and owls can hunt. And hugging the path I follow through this landscape, stands of trees for them to roost in. The setting, if not the light, seems ideal. Much of birdwatching is optimism. And in the ingredients laid out before me, I have cause to be cautiously optimistic.

The road I follow hugs the river carving its way through the estate. Barn owls often hunt along rivers. But the cover here is too dense. Though pared back beside the path, I'm still overarched by sycamore and beech, and laurels are rampant. The setting is eerie. It feels sticky and claustrophobic, a highway of humidity. Everything is strangled by ivy. Even the corpses of dead trees by the path are still constricted by its cruel embrace. From somewhere over the trees, the quack of a mallard is the only reminder that the river is nearby.

To my relief, the trees soon break. The golf course resumes; a brace of late golfers drag buggies up the rolling slopes. Grass grows luscious by the path around me, a bedrock for barn owls. It is tanned at the tips, swept over by the comb of the wind. The shoots of dock leaves are rusty red amid the grass engulfing the trees, now standing apart in a broken stretch of woodland.

Over my shoulder, Tyrconnell Tower, its merlons bristling like a crown, looms atop a hill, buttressed by copses on either side.

Golfers aside, the estate is abandoned to the coming night. As shadows lurch from the trees and visibility plummets, I try to enter the mind and senses of a barn owl. Sound is the currency of the night. There's no hope of spotting a rat or a mouse now. But every rustle is a giveaway. Any call is either fearless or foolish. From somewhere in the trees a lonely woodpigeon coos, making the most of the silence. Much further out, traffic forms a constant backdrop, like the drone of an uilleann pipe.

The light keeps fading, but I can just about discern movement as I follow the pathway trailing around the estate. Little white flags flicker from greens on the golf course, misleading my eyes eager to pick out the underwing of a barn owl. Four gulls pass overhead; even they are afraid to break the silence of the twilight.

About me, the rolling expanse of grass weaves like a double helix through formidable walls of trees. The ash and sycamore are conjoined by horse chestnuts, green flails weighing down many-fingered leaves; ready for autumn, ripe for the shed. With their presence, the estate feels equally suited to barn and long-eared owls. Both are meant to be present here, dominating the neighbouring domains of grass and woodland by night, sinking back into the foliage or old buildings by day.

I became more intimate with the landscape of north Kildare during my student days in Maynooth. At the time, I can remember thinking the scenery here dull. Cut adrift from the sea, it lacked the jagged cliffs broken by coves and charming beaches that defined the eastern border of Wicklow.

Then there are the mountains – or lack thereof. If I were to describe the land here in one word, it would be flat. In Wicklow, you're never that far from a mountain. Even in the towns, there's usually one or two in sight. In the countryside they're unavoidable. They make no mark on the plains of north Kildare; the distant hills I can see here are a pitiful imitation, sawn off and smoothed out halfway up. But this open expanse is what makes Kildare prime horse country. It's also what made it ideal for barn owls. They have no great love for mountains, and so a pancaked landscape is ideal.

Suddenly, punching proud above the trees that dominate the horizon, I see the unmistakable spire of Connolly's Folly, narrowing to a pyramid at its summit. It dates from 1740, when it was built to provide employment for local people during a time of famine. Subsequent famines would see similarly useless structures raised across the country, empty towers or roads to nowhere carved through bracken and gorse. I often wondered if the men who built such things could take any pride in their work, knowing it had no use once finished. Or maybe desperation left no place for pride, and the promise of food was enough to keep them going.

Since its construction, the folly has come to fill a sinister void in local lore. According to a website that college friends of mine happened upon, running around the folly backwards a certain number of times would summon the devil himself. (Those same friends attempted this without success.) Regardless of its supernatural potency, it still strikes an imposing figure. Zigzagging streaks of cloud seem to emanate from it, as if to augment its otherworldly mystique. I contemplate it from afar, thinking how a barn owl's shriek would complete the aura of horror.

Further along and I see the much more imposing tower of a church, stabbing the skyline to counteract the evil flowing from the folly. Beside it, a few lights from Maynooth twinkle, fireflies in a vast forested plain. To the right and down a slope, Carton House, in all its majesty, plugs a gap in the trees.

On the grassy slope, without trees to shield me or birdsong to distract me, the wind traces the channels of my ears. The rain has held off, as I'd hoped; if there are barn owls about, they'll be hunting tonight. I wonder how the wind will affect their foraging, false rustles slithering through the grass throwing them off their hunt. Surely all of those finely tuned accoutrements of the barn owl can discern the difference? That or the owl gets pulled in a dozen directions by every drop of a leaf or twitch in the grass, no better than a moth chasing every light that crosses its path.

Following the path that loops around the estate takes me to Tyrconnell Tower, like a great chess rook alone on the board. Like the folly, it was built as a famine relief project, the hunger of past generations imprinted on the landscape. I circle it to take in its grandeur. Four-sided, its hollowed-out window frames are propped up by rusted bars, one or two panes outlasting the decay of time. Roofless, the grey sky above peers through the uppermost of the windows on each side. The door is blood red; even carved graffiti can't damage the paint.

Studying its desolate structure, I think it would make a perfect keep for barn owls. It's exactly the kind of building I'd always pictured them living in, a husk of a memory of an Ireland long gone. All I hear from the tower, though, are the bleats of young swallows, echoing within the tunnel formed by its walls. Their parents circle out from it, chasing each other, a final reconnaissance before the night closes in. I relax on the grass beneath the tower, shielded by it, tiny in its shadow. Here I watch the swallows, like inverse shooting stars above me; the death throes of a long, hot summer.

A half-moon rises, melting out of the sky. With no mountains to demand your attention, it's easier to appreciate the textures of the sky here. By now, a great mass of cloud has swept in; a duvet covering north Kildare for the night. Like some haunted beacon, the only light seems to seep from the folly, a pink haze meandering through grey. Kildare can feel so suburban at times. But I've always known there were pockets of serenity here, islands of blissful solitude. This crossroads of place and time is one of them.

Down the slope, towards the mass of broadleaved trees, short shrieks come suddenly. The cry is trifold, the first note deeper than the two that follow. The call is unfamiliar to me; it's not the elongated, guttural hiss I'd come to expect of a barn owl. It's not the deep, resonating hoot of a long-eared owl either, or the greasy squeak that their chicks make when hungry. As soon as I'm tempted to make for the woods and investigate, it stops. I wait. The maker desists, and refuses to break the stillness with its flight. An apparition of the ears, a deception of the night tempting me to run aground in the forest as darkness fills the void behind me. I decline to follow it.

As I descend towards Carton House, boots on the gravel path stir jackdaws in a panic from an oak tree. A bat, a true emissary of the night, forms my escort. It cuts like a laser through sycamore seeds spiralling towards the ground, teardrops for a summer in retreat.

Autumn is on its way.

JAY

Phoenix Park

A lion roars.

I've just returned from Africa, from game parks home to actual wild lions. And yet, the only place in which I've ever heard a lion roar is Dublin's Phoenix Park. Dublin Zoo, at the heart of the park, has reared more captive lions than any other. This is where the roar comes from, the male of the pride proclaiming dominion over his man-made domain. Alas, no young champion should seek to take his land and title. But his reign is all the more peaceful – and his life in captivity all the longer – for it.

Entering the park, the Wellington Monument, the tallest obelisk in Europe, greets you. As a boy I could remember the rush of excitement every time I saw it, for this meant that the zoo was close. It wasn't until much later that I was awoken to the other animals contained within Phoenix Park. It's the largest enclosed park in any European city; the zoo consumes only a fraction of it. The captive animals might be the big draw, but there's space aplenty here for wild things too.

The most charismatic of its wild denizens are the fallow deer, descendants of the original herd introduced in the 1600s. In late autumn they make a spectacle of themselves in the grassy stretches of the park. The does gather in herds and the stags run to and fro, trying to corral them. As well as the antlers, the stag also re-grows his Adam's apple each rutting season. It is this that he slides up and down his throat to make the guttural belch with which to woo females and ward off rivals. The clash of antlers is left as a last resort.

Rutting season apart, there's more subtle wildlife to be savoured in the park. As I progress along the road leading from the main entrance, trees conjoin the path. The grass between and behind them is lined with woodpigeon getting in their grazing before the park swells with urbanites. If I pass too close, they take off as one, with an applause of wings, fanning out through the trees.

Of course, crows abound in the park, as they do almost everywhere in Ireland. Hooded crows purr from the high branches. Jackdaws cling to fences beside the zoo entrance, awaiting the first visitors of the day and the food they'll bring with them. And from the deeper veins of forest, the undulating coo of the pigeons is spiked by the cackle of magpies.

But it's an altogether different crow that draws me to the park in late September. It's a bird that fascinated me as a child – and has eluded me ever since. A creature with deep roots stretching back to Ireland's forested past, and possessed of an intellect we're only now starting to comprehend.

●●●

One of the formative experiences that piqued my interest in birds was when my father explained the order of Irish crows. What until then had been a uniform company of black, grey and white suddenly became a vivid family of birds, each with their own unique traits.

The raven, the king of the crows, towers over the others. Then comes the hooded crow, a meeting of grey and black, with that stout bill as at home tearing through carrion as it is sifting through the detritus of the sea. The rook is the most common of the lot, probably the bird most people think of when they think 'crow'. Seemingly omnipresent with the rook is the jackdaw, smaller and more rounded. The magpie is the most elegant but with a sinister reputation, harbinger of misfortune and glutton for shiny things. The chough is the rarest of the lot, a bird of wild cliffs and mountainsides, combing for insects with that curved red bill.

And then there's the jay.

Crow and colourful don't often go together. When you think corvid, you think monochrome. The jay is anything but. Tan encircles the flanks and back, with brilliant electric blue scaling on the upper wings. A white forehead streaked with charcoal black offers more contrast to this vivid palette. The black on the tail, wings and moustachial stripes pay homage to the uniform more common among crows, signifying membership of the clan. You'd think its resplendent regalia were compensating for the mediocrity of its relatives. It makes the jay one of the most strikingly colourful birds we have. It's a shame, therefore, that it's often not as in evidence as its more rambunctious relatives, relegated to patches of forest that cling on across the country.

What the corvids so often lack in colour, they compensate for with intellect. Crows are easily among the most intelligent of birds. It is this that has let them adapt to an increasingly human world with an ease few other birds can match. Granted, the jay may not accept bread or terrorise gardens with the belligerent confidence of the jackdaw or magpie, but its brainpower is no less striking.

Captive birds have shown this in experiments. They were tasked with inserting stones into tubes filled with water, the displaced liquid pushing a parcel of food higher and higher until it was within reach. With striking aptitude, the jays soon got to grips with this concept. In so doing they demonstrated a capacity for tool-use on par with primates, our closest relatives in the animal kingdom.

At no time of year is this intellect better demonstrated in the wild than now in the autumn. This is when the jay must call on that formidable mind to provision for the winter ahead.

Ripened after a long growing season, the oak trees finally release their crop, a glut of acorns peppering the leaf-litter below. With such a bounty, the jay can be forgiven for eating its fill. But with a forecasting that would make the most frugal of farmers proud, the bird then systematically caches acorns in buried spots around the forest. In so doing, it guarantees itself enough food to see out the lean winter ahead, when food will almost certainly be harder to come by. The oaks are also unpredictable in their munificence; not every tree will deliver every season, so the jays need to provision while they can.

The intellect inherent in this cannot be overstated. It shows a degree of forethought on par even with chimpanzees. Small wonder some scientists have taken to calling jays 'feathered apes'.

Imagine, for a second, you were told that the supermarkets would stop stocking their shelves tomorrow. You needed to load up on food for a few months to come – or else face starvation. Softened by modern convenience, with what degree of accuracy could you (or me) predict your future calorific requirement, store it (without the help of a freezer) and (crucially) keep it hidden from anyone else who might have eyes on it?

The last stipulation is a real concern for the jay. The forests are awash with creatures that would make short work of a buried stash of acorns. Other jays – pilferers – are among the worst offenders. They are happy to devour the fruits of another bird's excavations. But the more prudent jays have smartened up to this trick. They try to keep their caches out of sight if a pilferer is around. It's even been proven that jays are more cautious about where they bury their food if they suspect a pilferer might be watching. This need for covert collection and storage of food is one reason why jays are so furtive, and often difficult to observe.

All of this speaks to another dimension of intelligence, one often not credited to birds. Stashing food is one thing. But the real catalyst for greater intelligence in many animals (not least of all humans) is understanding conspecifics: determining intentions, deciphering friend from foe, forging alliances and seducing a mate. The jay not only needs to bury its acorns, but must deduce the designs of other jays on said acorns and cache them in a spot where they won't be easily found.

This keen intuition into the thoughts of other jays isn't rooted solely in cynicism. It also comes into play in the mating arena. The male jay uses food to court his mate. He does this by watching what food she consumes, and then bringing her a new food item that he hasn't yet seen her eat. In this way, the male must not only anticipate his own future nutritional needs, but also those of the female he's trying to woo. Doing this requires knowledge of the 'other' as a distinct entity, an awareness of beings beyond oneself. This comes as second nature to humans, but is rarely observed in the natural world, even among our mammal relatives.

For all their formidable memory, the jays (including the pilferers) never get to some of their acorns. They can hide up to five thousand in a season, but only recall where around 75 per cent of them are hidden. This is a blessing for the oak tree. This serendipitous slip of the mind is the price the oak extorts from the jay for all that food it provides. Buried beyond the reach of herbivores – and beyond the constricting embrace of its parents' branches or roots – the acorn can germinate in peace. This way, the jay helps to spread the oak seeds – and the forest.

I try to peel back the roads and buildings, the towns and homesteads, to a time after the ice and before the ravages of civilisation, when Ireland was covered in forest almost from edge to edge. Oaks were among the staple trees in these verdant woodlands, along with the retinue of other plants and creatures that come with them. An oak is an ecosystem. Every tree harbours hundreds of species of invertebrates, themselves nurturing dozens of birds. The seeds and saplings are fodder for squirrels and deer, the branches are highways for pine martens. Through all this, the jay is the agent of the oaks, gardener of the forest, aiding its advance year after year. Even the most elusive of creatures can shape the landscape around them. Without jays, would Ireland's once famed oak forests have ever come into being, and the floral and faunal makeup of our island looked a whole lot different?

Jays in Ireland are even more special because they comprise a unique race, found nowhere else in the world. The Eurasian jay has a wide range – from Ireland to Japan, with dozens of races across that massive territory. Some of them are strikingly different from others. Overall, the Irish race is darker in profile than its British or continental counterparts, and other subtle details of the face can also tell them apart. What advantage all this incurs in the bird's Irish domain, I do not know. Perhaps it is something lost in the long genetic legacy of jays on this island, stretching back thousands of years to the first jays that followed the forests here as the ice retreated, and stayed cut adrift when the melting glaciers filled in the Irish Sea. Sundered from sedentary jays elsewhere, perhaps, with the slow passage of time, they would eventually have evolved into a species all of their own: Ireland's only endemic bird. Maybe they will yet.

The jay is not in trouble in Ireland – yet. But if it had a heyday here, it's certainly over now. Ireland is not the forested country it once was. Once upon a time, around 80 per cent of this island was pure, native woodland. Centuries of harvesting and clearance have wrought a shocking ruin to our forests. Oak was cherished for its fine finishes, and as an excellent substrate for furniture. Necessity also played a part; homes had to be warmed during winter, and fires had to be fuelled somehow.

Old oak woodlands were decimated, but never replaced. Now, less than 1 per cent of Ireland has native forest cover, the lowest of any country in Europe. That's a lot less space for oaks to reach their magnificent potential – and jays to flourish in their shadows.

Many of the forests we now have are a poor substitute for what was lost. Those conifer plantations clinging to mountainsides across the country are next to useless to the jay, and to many of the other native species squeezed into a smaller and smaller space. Oaks can't take root in the poor, denuded soil of our high mountains, and take three times longer to mature than many conifers. For commercial foresters looking to make a return on investment, it was an easy choice which tree to plant.

Crows, as a group, have shown a remarkable adaptability to the human world. But of all our crows, it is the jay that has succumbed most to specialisation. It's a temptation that entices all species, often to great success – and ruin thereafter. The jay's bond with the oaks was profitable when the woods ranged far and wide. But on an island increasingly without wild woodland, can it adapt fast enough to hold on?

•••

It's no surprise, given its history, that the Phoenix Park should offer sanctuary to jays, respite from the urbanisation happening all around. The park was initially carved out of the countryside by the Duke of Ormonde in the seventeenth century. His aim was to preserve a portion of wilderness – not out of charity, but as a prime hunting ground for visiting royalty. It was for this purpose that the fallow deer were released into the park. It was also stocked with pheasants and partridges for shooting, though the latter are now absent altogether.

It wasn't until sometime later, in 1747, that the park would finally open to the public. Since then, it has gone on to play a paramount role in the heritage and lore of Dublin, hosting two popes and concerts beyond count, to say nothing of those who came before. Winston Churchill spent his formative childhood years here. It was in the Phoenix Park that he first witnessed soldiers drilling; some suspect that this planted the seed of martial interest in him.

My journey here begins in the early morning. The road through the park is already weighed down with parked cars. There's scarcely an empty space to be seen. As I trace its outline on the footpath, I'm eclipsed by joggers, limbering up or slogging past me in luminous jackets. An autumn chill saturates the air.

Trees loom over me as I follow the main route through the park. Ash, beech, horse chestnut ... but no oaks. In dismay I survey the leaves of every tree I cross. None fit the lobed profile I'm looking for. True, jays aren't bound to oaks for dear life. But if you want to find them, oak trees are your safest bet.

The path beneath me offers more reason for hope. The trees I walk past may not fit the profile I need, but their nuts and seeds are strewn across the ground. Horse chestnuts squeeze and burst underfoot, lime green rusting into brown. The exposed nuts have begun to peel off their polished chocolate coating, unveiling the white succulence beneath. Autumn has taken hold of the deciduous trees. The harvest season has begun. I'm hoping the oaks, when I find them, are as generous.

A booming voice soon informs me why there are so many joggers in the park. Unbeknownst to me, this is the day of the Dublin Half Marathon. Over a loudspeaker, the voice reads out the honour roll, the list of past winners and names of runners come from far and wide to partake. In between, he boasts how the Canadian Prime Minister has not returned to Ireland since his Irish counterpart ran him ragged around the Phoenix Park last year. There's a building buzz about the park; every trail is pregnant with joggers now, converging on the starting point. It makes for a jovial atmosphere, but I just hope the birds of the park aren't frightened into hiding by the commotion.

The routes through the park soon converge, and I peel off in the direction of Ashtown Castle. No more cars can follow me, and I'm left to progress on foot. Here, at last, are oak trees in all their glory, with only a few ash in between. Oaks of all ages swarm around the path, from saplings wreathed in mesh to ward off the deer to knotted veterans of centuries past. The oldest are festooned with fungus on their lower trunks, like half-moon slabs of buttered toast.

Many lobed leaves parachute slowly to the ground amid the crackling of twigs. It's hard at times to tell if this is merely the will of the trees or the ripples of animals moving unseen through the canopy. Jays? Perhaps. But whatever the culprit, it escapes my vision.

A road wrapped in white metal fence leads to the park's visitor centre, ballooning around the old Ashtown Castle. The castle was raised by the Knights Hospitaller in the 1400s, having been granted these lands some centuries before. It was from here that they sought to gather funds, money to finance future designs on the Holy Land.

Trees curve out from either side of the visitor centre like a bow, embracing a lake of grass. It is slightly quieter here, away from the brewing chaos of the marathon. The paths through the aisles of trees are the domain of dog walkers. But for the most part, this space is left to the birds.

Above, the perpetual dual between conifers and broadleaves that defines so many Irish woodlands is in full battle. No clear victor is apparent, but it doesn't seem to bother the creatures that move through their branches and forage in their shadows. Grey squirrels leave shivering leaves in their wake. The understory is awash with birdsong. The grating whistle of the long-tailed tit surrounds me, seeming to hollow through my head at times. Robins make a fuss of every perceived intrusion, and set the park ringing with their alarm calls as blackbirds toss leaves on the ground. A wren dips in and out of the briars and fallen logs, looting the detritus of the wind for food.

Even in narrow strips of trees like this, the claustrophobic nature of woodland birding sets in: the alarm calls; the sudden bursts of flight; the intuition, eons old, that dozens of suspicious eyes are zeroing in from all angles. Forests can't help but impress upon you the paranoia of living within them. Nooks and crannies abound for your quarry (or foe) to hide in. At times, even the trees themselves seem to conspire against you. One huge hazel in particular seems to rustle every time I draw near, the little creatures in its branches a private militia, giving voice to its irritation.

Part of me wonders if even the very birdsong around me is an illusion. Are the calls even real? Or are the jays, masterful mimics as they are, making a mockery of me from the branches, pranksters taunting me with a soundboard.

The genius of the jay also manifests in its mastery of the calls of other birds it shares the forest with. Even experienced birdwatchers can find it hard to tell them apart. Particularly impressive are its imitations of raptors, which are thought to help it intimidate and confuse other birds when needed. Some jays will even copy human speech, or weave the motifs of suburban soundscapes (lawn mowers, crying babies, dripping taps) into their songs. Why jays do this isn't known for certain. Perhaps they are as adept at collecting sounds as they are acorns. But maybe this is a stash they just can't keep to themselves. Exotic vocalisations could be alluring to mates. Or the sounds the jay makes could be an expression of a personality and life history, not yet revealed in a form humans can fully understand.

Colour counts for little in the shade of the forest. The vivid patterning that adorns our tits and finches is black-washed by the shadows. One bird can rotate into another, its identity only crystalising once you get a good look at its shape.

And it's shape, not colour, that betrays my first jay.

At first I'm convinced it's just another jackdaw leading me astray. But as it flicks with grace through the fingers of a lower branch, the balance of tail and breast just isn't right. A quick glance through the binoculars clinches it. The resplendence is buried by the canopy, but the rings around the eyes and fine filigree of the face still reveal themselves, a memory of their true beauty etched beneath an opaque veneer.

The jay's woodland habits seem engrained even in the way it moves. It sweeps from branch to branch with an arboreal flourish hard to imagine for a bird of its size. This is no tit or goldcrest, able to tunnel through twigs without registering so much as a rustle. Yet there's something simian in the smoothness of it, and when it parts from the tree it does so with a silent flutter, not the graceless eruption of a woodpigeon. Another bird, perhaps its mate, follows it deeper into the undergrowth. Had it not moved, this second jay would have escaped my sight altogether, hidden right above my head.

Then, as if confident that I pose no threat, jays suddenly seem to appear out of nowhere. Another bird meanders through the branches of an oak further along the trail. Its beak is parted by an acorn. The jay is looking for the perfect opening to wedge it in, just tight enough to resist the hammering of its beak. It tries a few without success before graciously swooping onto a denuded branch right above my head. Here, if only for a few seconds, the elongated embrace of the oak leaves can't touch it. The lighting is far from perfect, but I can make out the soft tan that envelopes the flanks and brilliant white of the forehead.

Abandoning its enterprise, the jay swallows the acorn whole. Crop bulging, it takes flight. The bird itself is then swallowed by the forest.

Another oak – and another jay to tend to it. This one is too impatient to wait for the tree to part with its crop. Instead, it shows off its arboreal acrobatics, deftly hanging upside down as it teases the acorns from their sockets. I've seen rooks attempt this in the past, but never with the masterful dexterity on display here. Their bulk is too much for the twigs that terminate the oak branches, and they're forced to flap awkwardly to restore balance. The jay, the acorn professional, need only keep its wings half-open as a safety measure.

Then, with a flick, it's off, falling with grace. Elliptical wingbeats carry it in a smooth curve to alight atop a green fence post, acorn clamped in its bill. Here, for the first time, I get to take the bird in in its full majesty. Behind it, brooding laurels form a dark backdrop. Against them, the lucid colours of the jay make for handsome viewing, even in the half-light filtering down from the canopy. I try to capture it with my camera, to imprint the spectacle I behold. But the darkness of the undergrowth deceives the sensor, and the jay is shrouded in shadow, muted as the forest desires it to be. One concession to modernity and I'm punished. When I look up from the screen, the jay is gone.

I press on through the sliver of forest, conceited in thinking the jay can't elude me in such a small space. But the catalogue of shrubs that rub the knees of the oaks and horse chestnuts offer no shortage of places to hide. As I come close, the robins and blackbirds of the undergrowth kick off with their warning cries.

This time, though, an unfamiliar call joins them. A deep, rasping squawk; it feels as if it's summoned from the very bowel of the throat, a strain even on the twin vocal chords a bird is born with. It's the alarm call of a jay – no imitation, just the bird's true voice. It feels like far too sinister a sound to come from such a handsome creature; as close to a growl as I've yet heard from a bird. The thrushes and robins serve to alert others of a threat, but this feels like the threat itself; a warning from the depths of the wood, bidding ill will on any foolish enough to trespass. Satisfied with my day's exploits, I decide to heed the warning and trouble the forest creatures no further.

In pitifully few steps I'm back at the visitor centre, back into the world of paved walkways and manicured grass where trees are reduced to window dressing. The sky above, unbroken by leaves, is a uniform September grey; milk mixed through with a drop of tar. With an applause, the half-marathon begins.

HEN HARRIER

South Wexford

The colossal structures of the Vancouver skyline lend a perfect backdrop to a female northern harrier, crossing the road in front of our vehicle. My guide has spotted her, approaching the road from behind some trees to our right. He pulls over just in time for us to get out and find her in our binoculars, stroking the air with delicate wings as she winds across a stretch of suburban greenery. Her white rump, a trait she shares with her European counterpart, is the most striking feature as she disappears over some bushes in the distance.

It was a perfect start to my Canadian birdwatching trip – but also bittersweet. I had crossed a vast ocean – and continent – to catch sight of the North American cousin of Ireland's native hen harrier. A bird I had yet to see, despite innumerable visits to suitable winter quarters down through the years. It was a stain on my Irish birding record I just had to address.

•••

Even amongst Ireland's small collection of raptors, we're lucky enough to have some beauties. The red kite – a recent reintroduction – is always a pleasure in its russet outfit. All three of our falcons have their visual charms. And both of our eagles are bound to impress on sheer scale alone. But none of these birds can compare to the aesthetic splendour of the male hen harrier. He might not be the most boldly marked bird we have, but he is among the most eye-catching: a dapper grey, designed to stand out like a glint of silver on the vast moorlands on which he makes his summer home.

This is where the male flaunts his colour with one of the most renowned displays of any Irish bird, the fabled sky dance of the hen harrier. Taking wing over the heather, the male rises and falls like the mountains of his domain. In between he flicks and rolls, twisting about in the wind as if conceding to its will, before righting with ease to confirm his mastery of the sky. He may not have the bulk of a buzzard, or even of the female harrier. But he's all the more agile for it, and it is this that bequests him an aerial grace few raptors of his size can come close to matching.

It's during the sky dance that the male reveals himself to be more than a uniform grey, employing his monochrome highlights to their fullest extent. He takes advantage of what sunlight there is to flash his white belly across the landscape. As he folds in and out of the wind, he wields his black wing tips like two fans, their contrast accentuating his elegance and grace.

The male harrier employs the sky dance to seduce his mate, hypnotising her into submission with flamboyance. But this is no idle flourish. The dance demands the same agility the male will need to be a capable hunter – and provider. He'll need to be. Depending on food, and the availability of eligible mates, a male harrier can even be polygynous. This means he could have two families within his territory – two broods in need of his prolific hunting skills.

The hunting harrier can so often seem a benign waif, floating over the moor. Twisting and turning as it quarters, it seems almost an oversized butterfly, aimlessly carried along by the breeze. Its flight looks much less threatening than the purposeful circling of the buzzards, the bulky *buteos* with which harriers share so much of their global range. But it's no less effective.

Flying close to the ground, the harrier can employ another sense that many other diurnal raptors neglect: sound. Every rustle in the heather or the reeds could signpost a potential meal. And the harrier's face is designed to help it home in on the sounds of panicked prey, on any mistakes that might give away their position. The facial ruff of the harrier is like a halfway house between the disc of an owl and the more fearsome face typical of daylight raptors. It's not quite the sophisticated tracking device of the barn owl. But it works well enough to help channel any sounds into the harrier's ear. And, every once in a while, that rustle could be a bunting in the reeds or a rodent losing its nerve in the heather below.

This way, the bird 'harries' its victim into flight. Now, the harrier's agility comes into play to outmanoeuvre it. The lighter male harrier is more adept at catching birds; the female prefers to hunt over denser vegetation, where her greater size can help her in snuffing out small mammals.

Unlike the barn owl, the harrier doesn't have the veil of the night to hide it. Given this, it has to be tactful in its approach, using every crease in the terrain to conceal itself before the final pounce. This is another advantage of hugging the ground when on the hunt. Being within earshot of its target, and camouflaged by the bumps and foliage of the landscape, a harrier can find and finish prey beyond the radar of other raptors soaring high above.

In winter, our harriers are easier to see as they disperse from dancing arenas in the uplands to winter abodes in coastal sites around the country. Their numbers are supplemented by blow-ins from abroad, to whom Ireland's relatively mild winters offer respite. This is when the hen harrier becomes the great menace of the wetlands, putting the same surveillance techniques that served it well on the moors to deadly effect in cornering prey hiding amongst the reeds.

●●●

A white statue of the Virgin Mary stands proud at the entrance to the island named in her honour. Her golden crown makes a perch for jackdaws, which take off as soon as we approach. They're the first indication that now, when the pilgrimage season is over, Our Lady's Island, in the southeast corner of County Wexford, resumes its regular duty as a safe haven for birds.

Dad is with me as I embark on a day's harrier hunting. I'm hoping he'll be a good-luck omen. He likes to boast of seeing a hen harrier on Bray Head many moons ago. Maybe he can summon another one today. There's also my competitive side to consider; he's had a harrier over me for far too long.

If the hen harrier is one of the holy grails of Irish birding, then it's well placed in so hallowed a place as Our Lady's Island. 'Island', though, is a misnomer. The piece of land that juts into Lady's Island Lake is no island but a peninsula, bulging at the end to give the illusion of sovereignty from the mainland. It's the oldest Marian shrine in the country, and among the most revered.

True theologians doubt the Marian credentials of the island; it's disputed whether or not an apparition appeared here. But the appeal of Our Lady's Island, propped up by its serene setting, ensured its popularity for pilgrimage never waned.

While other of Ireland's sacred sites were proscribed during the days of the Penal Laws, oppressed Catholics were allowed to flock to Our Lady's Island to indulge in what divinity they could find here. They likely weren't the first. Pagan ruins suggest this corner of south Wexford attracted revellers even before Ireland was welded to Christendom. Who knows what kind of spirits the druids once tried to invoke before Ireland's holy sites, possessed of a tranquillity that transcended faiths, found themselves pledged to a new god.

The isolation to be found here even sheltered a dialect unique to this corner of Ireland. Wexford was where the Norman conquest of the island began, and Yola, as the dialect was known, descended from the very first English brought to Ireland by the Normans all those centuries ago. Shaped by other linguistic influences, it survived as a spoken tongue in this part of south Wexford right up until the 1800s – Our Lady's Island is believed to have been its last holdout. Even now, occasional licks of Yola still cling on in the local patter; most notably, '*quare*' stands in for 'very' in much of Wexford to this day.

Unlike Yola, the appeal of Our Lady's Island could not be confined to this corner of the southeast. The island's renown spread far beyond Irish shores. It was esteemed even at the highest echelons of the Catholic hierarchy. In 1607, Pope Paul V promised indulgences to any pilgrims who honoured the Fast of the Assumption (15 August) and the Feast of the Nativity of Our Lady (8 September) here. The window between the two feasts is considered the 'most meritorious' time to visit the island – for healing, if not for birding. A visit could cure all manner of ailments.

In moving around Ireland between seasons in search of birds, I feel I have come by the two poles of the spirit world: Tory Island, where misfortune was unleashed on unlucky sailors; and here, at the opposite end of the country, a place of reverence and redemption.

Worshippers went to great lengths to court salvation on the island, as seventeenth-century accounts attest:

> And there doe penance, going bare-leg and bare foote, dabbling in the water up to the mid leg, round the island. Some others goe one foote in the water, the other on dry land, taking care not to wet the one nor to tread dry with the other. But some great sinners goe on their knees in the water around the island and some others that are greater sinners yet, goe three times round on their knees in the water.

To this day, August and September still see thousands of worshippers descend on the island. For many years my grandmother was among them. Once, she brought me back a souvenir stone from the island, a token that's held a place on my bookshelf ever since. My parents tell me they brought me here to see her on pilgrimage as a young boy, but too much has happened in the intervening years for me to remember. I look forward now to tracing her footsteps, to enjoying the sights she once saw, even if our end goals are not the same.

Our Lady's Island is a special place for birds as well as worshippers. As with other renowned birding spots in south Wexford, the lake is a draw for winter visitors. Most winters, a hen harrier or two is among them.

As we set off in search of that harrier, the islands (the true islands) of Lady's Island Lake are overshadowed by lapwings, swirling like the undulation of some great sea slug. They land periodically to unite with the wigeons and black-headed gulls, forming living jetties that give greater reach to the little islands.

The islands are joined by step stones of swans, mute swans mostly, but also some whoopers, honking to give voice to their presence. Whoopers are wild by nature; perhaps because of their migratory habits, they haven't conceded to suburbia as easily as mute swans have. I've never gotten as close to wild whoopers as I have here. Maybe the comfort the mute swans feel around people has infected the whoopers, and they no longer think of nearby birders as a threat.

In summer, mute swans are fiercely territorial, chasing off even benign interlopers with wings cupped in a threat display. But the necessities of winter bring out a camaraderie in them. There's no animosity between birds on Our Lady's Island. As the mutes and whoopers feed side by side, their upended tails form white cones bobbing in threes and fours. And when they take off it's with a great wheezing of wings, like the spinning of some huge boomerang around the lake.

Seeing the whoopers back here gives some sense of an ending to my journey, my birding year coming full circle. I saw them when looking for partridges at Lough Boora back in March, when they were fattening up for the flight to Iceland. Now the breeding season is over, and they're back on Irish lakes and fields to wait out the winter once again.

Though it's not raining or cold, there's no doubt that winter is at hand now. The whoopers aren't the only sign. Grey clouds lair on top of one another like overlapping sheets of armour. Light can break through at only one weak point in the scaling, but where it does it sets the lake shimmering in an arc behind the crowned statue of Mary.

The pilgrim path makes for flat, easy walking around the island. I'm happy to see that it borders patchy reed beds, shimmering in the breeze: perfect hunting spaces for a wintering harrier. For now, though, the only predator I can see is a kestrel, static in the air, waiting for the denizens of the reeds to reveal themselves. Between the reeds, the shore of the island is rocky, and lathered with white foam like the froth blown off a beer. Occasional boats lie tethered to the shore. Aside from that, the human influence on the island is largely arcane. Most haunting is an old church, roofless and eroded by the centuries. Local people, fleeing the advancing Cromwell, took shelter in it in 1649. The church was burned, and the roof torn from it. The Augustinians, who tended the church at that time, were butchered. Mass has not been celebrated in the ruined structure since.

For all its tranquillity, the island is very small. Dad returns to the car after one lap. I decide to do another, in the hope of picking up something I might have missed before. Alone, I start to survey the far shores of the lake, hoping a harrier will materialise out of the countryside. Off the north end of the island, a huge assemblage of coots stains the water black. It's as if the shimmering white of the swans is too much for the lake, and an injection of darkness is needed to restore some balance.

Even someone devoid of faith can appreciate the peacefulness to be found here. This is not the summer silence I enjoyed in Connemara, with no relieving breeze to be had. It's as close to silence as you'll get in an Irish winter, the workings of the wind the only noise. It carves an atmosphere that's almost eerie; a pensive meditation, like the aftermath of some great battle – or a transitory truce waiting to be shattered. Every once in a while, a passing car or the sudden barking of a dog adds an anthropic flavour to the soundscape. For the most part, though, it's serene: an island of peace, if not of geography.

I keep my eyes peeled for the predator to bring some welcome chaos to the island. I figure it'll come from yonder, where the water surrenders to the farms and low hills of Wexford. A brown mass hunched over by the lake shore has me convinced it's a harrier, until a zoomed-in photograph confirms it to be a buzzard. Further afield, I make out two distant specs that I determine to be raptors. The first seems to be another kestrel, pausing mid-air as if frozen in suspended animation. The other rises in and out of the fields, scaring – or, dare I say it, harrying – a flock of starlings into flight. It looks bigger than a falcon, and is looping and banking in atypical fashion for a buzzard. But it's too far off to pin down the ID.

Even with these tantalisingly opaque views, an inexplicable euphoria comes over me. I can sense a harrier is close. I feel it. It's like a message being wordlessly conveyed to me, welling up from within the island itself. Maybe it was here yesterday. Or maybe it's somewhere else in the patchwork of lakes and reed beds that pepper south Wexford. In the days before I came here, I had even been visited in a dream by a male harrier. This sense of an impending harrier could be the waking manifestation of that. But maybe it's a false flag, a delusion. I'm not immune to them when looking for birds. Eagles turn out to be buzzards, merlins morph into kestrels. Serene as it is here, maybe my hunt for harriers should have been focussed elsewhere.

Though small, the natural curves of the island are still bulbous enough to conceal surprises. As I round one, I'm reminded not to focus too much on a distant prize to the neglect of the beauty right in front of me. Atop the silver water of the lake are as many swans as I've ever seen in my life. There are hundreds of them. And in the air, lapwings and godwits rampant.

Our Lady's Island may not be the best site for harriers, but it's a tremendous place for birds.

●●●

While the male harrier is on the hunt, it is the female – larger, stronger, and much better camouflaged by her bland browns among the heather – who guards the nest in spring. For the first few weeks after the chicks have hatched, she only takes to the sky to execute another of the hen harrier's renowned aerial manoeuvres: the food pass. Returning from a successful foray, the male tempts the female to take flight. She rises to meet him, rolling onto her back to demand his catch fill her talons. Sometimes, a brief chase ensues, as if the male is reluctant to part with his prize – even to his mate. This is when the difference between the sexes is at its clearest; she can be more than 40 per cent heavier than her mate, and the colour disparity is amongst the starkest of any raptor. A novice birder could be forgiven for thinking they were two different species, the larger mobbing the smaller. But inevitably the male relents, discarding his kill to the wind. Her leg jabs forward, like the strike of a cobra, to seize the prey before swooping back to the nest.

It's thought that harriers do this to make sure the food ends up in the talons it was intended for. A misplaced meadow pipit or rodent could easily become lost in the heather if the male just dropped it. While a meal could scarcely be mislaid in the treetop nest of a red kite or buzzard, the harrier nest is but a small depression on the ground, surrounded by a sea of heather and bracken.

The nest, by tradition, was made amongst the vegetation that once predominated in the Irish uplands. However, hen harriers have taken to young conifer plantations better than some of the other birds they share the mountains with in summer (notably the red grouse). Many birds now nest in nascent evergreen woodlands. But this only suits the harrier to a point. Trees grow tall, forests with them. The hen harrier is, at its heart, a bird of open spaces. This is not a creature of the trees. And so, as many of Ireland's conifer plantations have begun to mature, and the branches close in around them, harriers find themselves squeezed out of this space.

Like many Irish raptors, the harrier also fell afoul of human persecution. Much as prey species will react with fear or hostility to the sight of a quartering harrier, so too did generations of gunmen.

Although shooting is not the problem it was in the nineteenth century, habitat loss remains a very real concern for our harriers. The montane moorland harriers rely on for breeding has been undermined over the centuries, stripped away by turf cutting, tree planting and farming. Some of it has also been burned in a bid to bring more virility to the soil. Harriers not only need vegetation to shield themselves, but also to act as false cover for the creatures they like to feed on. Grass trimmed or burned down almost to the nub is no good to them. As a result, breeding harriers are now confined to a few remaining pockets of suitable habitat, primarily in the southwest, where the uplands are much as they once were.

This has all amounted to a sharp decline in harrier numbers in Ireland. Even in areas set aside for the species' protection, the number of harriers fell by more than a quarter between 2005 and 2015. As of this writing, there are believed to be fewer than two hundred pairs of breeding hen harriers left on the entire island. In recent times, incentives have been launched to encourage farmers to tend their lands in a manner compatible with hen harriers. Only time will tell if this is enough to save the species here.

●●●

A few detours. A close call with a fearless sheepdog. The car left muddied by damp country lanes, boreens that seem bound for nowhere. At the end of it all, we emerge at Tacumshin Lake.

The lake isn't as well signposted as Our Lady's Island. It doesn't draw legions of worshippers every year. There's no spiritual dimension to Tacumshin; its only appeal is the wild. It's a Mecca for birders. The lake serves as a staging post for rare passage migrants as well as a winter haven for visitors from the far north. Combined, they make for one of the most renowned birdwatching spots in Ireland – though few outside such circles have even heard of it.

This is my very first time at Tacumshin. I don't have the wellington boots recommended for such a site; though it looks calm when we arrive, the lake can be deceptive, rising with the tide to swallow up more of the shore. But I decide to venture off as far as I can.

I leave Dad in the car; he's seen enough for one day, and is probably more concerned with how we're going to get out of here with the paint job intact. I set off on my own, following the contours of the shoreline, shoes sinking into squelchy grass.

Spread out before me, Tacumshin Lake, wrapped in reed beds. At once it both cuts into and concedes to the countryside around it, pinned down by low-lying fields, buttressed by a ridge of sand on the far side. Tacumshin is one of only two lakes in Ireland to be separated from the sea in this way; the other is its sister lake engulfing Our Lady's Island. Both are more lagoon than lake.

At first, the complexion of the birdlife here seems much as it was there. The lake is weighed down with swans, both mute and whooper. Cruising between them are small sorties of scaup, like rubber ducks dipped in tar. Little grebes bubble up from beneath the surface of the lake. But beyond the placid toings and froings on the water, there seems to be a nervousness in the birds here that wasn't present at Our Lady's Island. It's writ large in the restlessness of the lapwings and frequent panicked cry of the curlew, in the masses of waders flowing about on the far shore of the lake. The birdlife is on edge, expecting an attack to come at any second.

I scan the far bank to investigate. That's when I see her, all brown from afar, long elastic wingbeats broken by bouts of gliding. I call it her; young male harriers are also brown, but I like to think this one's a she. There are ways to tell the genders apart, even if the male has yet to grow into his silvers, but this bird is moving at such speed and at such a distance I'll just have to assume.

I feel I've overcome the will-o'-the-wisps that tempted me astray on Our Lady's Island, the false harriers concealed in the form of a buzzard or far-off kestrel. This bird is also some way off, but not enough to obscure its identity. If Our Lady's Island was the test, purging me of my delusions, this is the reward. All the searching, all the dreaming, for this.

She flutters low over the reed beds and fields. Now and then she arcs upwards to contrast herself against the grey sky. In my delirium she's like a siren; I feel myself inextricably drawn to her. Eyes glued to my binoculars, I stride closer and closer to the lake shore until common sense stops me sinking into it.

The harrier continues to fold in and out of the fields in the distance. Concealing herself in the creases of south Wexford, I lose her and find her again. Then she's buried in lapwings. They rise as one, a great maw to consume their tormentor.

JACK SNIPE

North Bull Island

'**N**o lads. This is a really stupid idea.'

It felt like no matter how many times I repeated those words, I was going to end up on North Bull Island. And I did.

It was approaching 4 a.m. by the time we arrived at the bridge connecting the island to the mainland. The moon was veiled; the sun had yet to stir. The never-dinning lights of Dublin were all that guided the way.

The long walk to the bridge took us through a desolate suburban landscape, far removed from the pulsating nightlife of the nearby city centre. A brace of insomniac cyclists, weaving past empty playgrounds and barren bandstands, were the only company we found on the pathway that traced the edge of Dublin Bay. Beyond this, the low tide had unsheathed vast mudflats. Streams slithered through these on their way to the pure black waters of the bay beyond.

Even with an evening's worth of beer enjoyed, my birding instincts did not desert me entirely. Herring gulls, omnipresent on the streets of Dublin, occasioned us with their presence. In a city where the chip-shop castoffs of drunken partiers provide a bountiful food source, they've largely shed their diurnal nature, and seem equally at home foraging by lamplight. Their population has exploded in Dublin in recent decades (calls for a cull seem to surface every few months, citing horror stories of sandwiches snatched mid-air). Out on the mudflats, I could make out the silvery silhouettes of grey herons amid the murk. If we got too close, they would beat heavy wings into the air, a primeval honk joining the drone of distant traffic.

If a late-night ramble to North Bull Island had sounded like fun an hour ago, nervousness soon took hold. As the three of us made our way on foot across the bridge, we were worried by two packed cars roaring past, eager to make for the empty expanse of the island. But why?

It was this that convinced me that exploring North Bull Island at 4 a.m. was, indeed, a stupid idea. But egged on by a thirst for excitement, we persevered. As the bridge merged into the island, we stumbled from the tarmacked road onto undulating dunes. Tender underfoot, they made our progress even more taxing, until we arrived at a ridge crested with marram grass.

Beyond, we heard raised voices, angry and feral. They were too far for us to tell what they were saying, or even what language they were speaking. Michael braved a peek over the ridge, but saw nothing of interest. We hoped that, whoever they were, they saw nothing of interest in us as we beat a furtive retreat.

●●●

An isolated space within touching distance of the capital, North Bull Island (the 'North' is redundant) has an easy appeal to delinquents by night. And it's not just humans who savour the privacy it can provide. Among its diverse array of avian visitors, in winter Bull Island offers sanctuary to one of Ireland's most secretive birds: the jack snipe. It was the hope of seeing one that saw me make an early December return to the island.

Few people who've experienced an Irish winter look forward to it. It's not so much the rain that gets you. It's the cold, when the air around you is laden with the fog of your own breath. Above, dark clouds seem to blot out all sunlight – and all hope with it.

But birders have more reason to embrace the chill. This is when our coasts come alive with waders, welcomed back from breeding grounds to the far north: Scandinavia, Iceland, Siberia and even further. As harsh as an Irish winter is to us, it's balmy compared to the frozen onslaught these birds would face were they to remain among the taiga, where many waders (jack snipe among them) rear their young.

Only on its taiga breeding ground does the jack snipe shed its shyness. Each male lays claim to hectares of territory. He loops over his domain, proclaiming ownership with one of the weirdest calls in the entire symphony of Irish birds. It's been compared to the rhythm of a galloping horse. To me, it sounds vaguely like a UFO pulsing through space in a low-budget sci-fi flick. A shame, therefore, that the only jack snipe noise you're likely to hear in Ireland is a course bark as the bird breaks cover.

Breeding season is long over. Winter is when waders (jack snipe among them) throng by the thousands to mudflats like those at Bull Island. It's a truly immense journey to make for creatures the weight of a smartphone, but one the jack snipe is built for. Though smaller than the common snipe that lives here year-round, its wings are proportionally much longer; the hallmark of a long-distance migrant. The birds that winter in Ireland have it easy compared to those that complete the mammoth haul from northernmost Europe to sub-Saharan Africa, guided by magnetic fields beyond the scope of human senses.

Many waders are long-legged, allowing them to wade (hence the name) through the shallows in pursuit of prey. And it is this (and to avoid competing with each other) that has also led them to develop a staggering variety of bills with which to forage. The curlew is perhaps most iconic, with its long beak sublimely curved for prising lugworms from their burrows. Godwits, slim and elegant, have a straighter beak, and probe for prey that bit closer to the surface. The oystercatcher's orange instrument is sturdier still, adept at unlocking stubborn bivalves. Dunlins and knots, with short black bills, take what they can from just beneath the sand. And sanderlings, ebbing and flowing with each wave, collect all the sustenance they need from the flotsam served up by the sea.

The jack snipe is a short, squat creature. It can't forage in water of any depth. This, combined with its shy nature, sees it relegated to the recesses of the marsh. Here, away from the flocks congregating on the mud or open water, it can practice its bizarre feeding technique. As its bill jackhammers the mud for food, its entire body rocks up and down with the motion, as if the bird is balancing on springs. Most waders keep their bodies motionless as the bill gets to work. What benefit the jack snipe derives from involving its whole body in the process is unclear. Perhaps it becomes so immersed in its foraging that its whole being has to join in.

While most of our visiting waders feed communally, out in the open, the jack snipe is best at home hidden among reed beds, or skulking in long grass or wet ditches. It prefers to go unseen if it can, and its plumage has evolved to make sure it does: a streaky patchwork of straw and chocolate browns, highlighted with a green sheen when you catch it in good light. While many waders (godwits, knots, dunlins, sanderlings) shed their breeding finery for the winter, jack snipe maintain their stunningly cryptic camouflage year-round.

It's a colour combination that serves the snipe family well throughout their worldwide range. There are twenty-five or so species, none of them deviating much from this palette. Crouched among the reed beds they so often call home, it renders them all but invisible. Time and again I've startled a common snipe into flight while walking near the reeds at Broad Lough in Wicklow – the same reeds I'd just scanned with my binoculars, detecting nothing.

But even common snipe will at times feel at ease enough to feed in the open, probing their freakishly long bill into the mud for invertebrate prey. Jack snipe almost never do this. Their secretive nature makes them notoriously difficult to both study and survey, particularly here on their wintering grounds. Of all our regular waders, they are perhaps the most mysterious.

Staring out at the vast expanse of Bull Island, rising out of Dublin Bay like a sand-covered submarine, I know that finding such a tiny, well-hidden bird here will be a challenge. But few things worth seeing are easy to come by.

•••

As I make my way through the streets of Raheny, the north Dublin suburb adjacent to Bull Island, the sky above arcs from navy in the west to purple in the east, tempered by the rising sun. Before long, I emerge at the causeway, one of two footholds that connect the island to the mainland. The path, strewn with sand from the beach on the island, runs through mounds of grass like a paved valley. The sky above me is now a dull grey save a weak sliver where the milky rays of the sun have broken through. Against the off-light of early morning, gulls blackened, like the photo negatives of birds, their colours fuzzed and even reversed, fly past. In the distance, the lights of Dublin bleed into the murk.

To either side of the causeway stretch out the mudflats, broken by metallic-looking pools. Out on the mud, the chunky forms of brent geese are clumped in threes and fours, nibbling with half interest at the weeds laid out at low tide. Poles that emerge at odd angles from the mud are capped by hooded crows, frustrating my urge to see the merlins or peregrines that so often haunt coastal sites in winter. In the distance I hear the whistle of oystercatchers, and the echoing cries of curlews. The curlews are stretched out in a line to the left of the causeway, murmuring amongst themselves, a curlew moot. Their cries seem to rise and fall in unison, like so many sirens.

The boundaries of Dublin Bay have ebbed and flowed over the centuries. Were the Gaels and Norsemen who took to the field at Clontarf in 1014 to do battle at the same spot now, many of them would be fighting below the waves. Bull Island is just another consequence that the forces of erosion and deposition have had on this coast. Just 300 years ago, there were no sand dunes here for shy waders to shelter in or midnight delinquents to frequent.

Bull Island has nothing by way of bedrock. Its presence in the multi-million-year history of Dublin Bay is fleeting, just like that of the birds that overwinter here. Sand that was washed up this coast and deposited in the bay built up grain by grain. Coupled with the inclement weather, this rising sandbank, insidiously hidden by the sea, proved the ruin of merchant vessels plying the bay.

It wasn't until the nineteenth century that the carnage wrought by this submerged menace was finally addressed. The Act of Union that bound Ireland to Britain in 1801 brought with it a greater desire to harness the maritime potential of Dublin Bay. Charged with accomplishing this was William Bligh – a man who would later earn an enduring place in popular culture as the commander of HMS *Bounty*. After a thorough survey of the area, he drew up plans for a seawall to bisect the northern section of Dublin Bay. From 1818 to 1821, stone hewn from Dalkey at the far end of the bay was ferried here by barge and shaped into a wall by the labour of convicts. When they were finished, it jutted out nearly three kilometres into the Irish Sea.

Intentionally or not, this pier provided the crutch against which the growing Bull Island could support itself. Over the decades that followed, more and more sand built up to form the island that exists today. By 1900 it was around 4.5km long. It has piled on more bulk since then as the marram grass that took root in the sand helped shore up the island's surface.

Further out, salt marsh plants started spreading out over mudflats that now host brent geese and curlews. Wherever you get mudflats you find the worms and shellfish that flourish in intertidal zones. And where such creatures thrive, waders are rarely far away. By the 1930s, the island had attracted so many of them that it was named Ireland's first bird sanctuary. It's picked up even more prestigious accolades since then, now boasting UNESCO Biosphere status (shared with the rest of Dublin Bay).

As I progress along the causeway, the mudflats to my left are flecked with tufts of curved grass. But the grass has finally found more purchase on the open space to my right, with muddy troughs scooped through it sheltering redshanks that flush noisily if you get too close. They bob their heads up and down in a reflex motion, flashing pale bellies as if trying to seize your attention, only to take off in a panic once they succeed.

Approaching the island, a solitary building – itself an island in a sea of marram grass – is one of the few outposts of human endeavour to be seen. At its summit, a black wind vein tilts meekly from side to side, too forlorn to even spin. Beyond, the twin tips of the Poolbeg Towers, red stacked on top of white, shade into the clouds. Great Sugarloaf, that iconic landmark of my native county, is sublimely backlit by the rising sun, as if someone had traced a paintbrush dipped in orange just above its outline.

Finally arriving on the island, I find the ubiquitous marram grass swept over everything, combed over by the wind, bleached at the tips. Here, the calls of curlews are usurped by the japes of magpies. They perch on wooden pillars or the branches of low bushes, seeming to encircle me, as if in anticipation of some feast to come. Hooded crows, their bulkier cousins, swoop past me, heavy wingbeats like the pants of a large dog.

For all its impressive length, Bull Island is narrow by girth and easy to traverse. Following the road around through the mounds of marram grass, I soon emerge at the vast sweep of Raheny Strand, beloved by so many generations of Dubliners. People throng here in summer as a respite from the hectic life of the city. Even in December it provides a serene setting. Out to sea, a pair of brent geese are all that breaks the milky grey of the water. Dublin Bay is framed by Howth curling round to the north and Bray Head to the south. Along the strand, ecstatic dogs race up and down; it's like they don't know what to do with so much space, and so try to see all of it in the hopes that nothing of interest escapes them. In their exuberance, they scare a flock of oystercatchers into flight, beating their retreat in a cloud of black and white. Their owners jog by in their wake, jacketed and gloved to keep out the cold.

William Bligh's wall – now known as the Bull Wall – long, dark and thin, joins the horizon to the south. It's dwarfed by the distant tectonic contortions of the Wicklow Mountains. Towering above it, you'd think they were making a mockery of the petty precision of Bligh and the toil of all those convicts centuries ago. None of their efforts can match the monuments nature has carved out of this landscape. Closer to me, a ferry looms over the wall as it crawls out to sea.

Every few hundred yards, the sand to either side of me is blackened by hooded crows, ever eager to swoop on the munificence of the sea. But while they're confident enough to forage out here in the open, and the scenic beach walk to the Bull Wall is tempting, I know I won't find my quarry here. So I do an about-face in search of ditches and marshes; the slimy, shadowy places that jack snipe call home.

It doesn't take long to find what I'm after. As the sandy bulk of Bull Island erupted out of the Irish Bay, it provided more than just a space for Dubliners to sun themselves on summer days. The undulating surface lent itself perfectly to golf aficionados, and they've now shaped two of the capital's most renowned courses out of its surface. These are the only spaces on Bull Island where manicured lawns can be found, and the marram grass has been beaten back.

Crossing one of these, I emerge at a vast patchwork of swamp. By now, the cold has started to bite. The joints in my fingers seem to creek as I tighten my hands, and my glasses pixelate under the relentless flecking of rain. But I know I'm on the right path now. If there are jack snipe to be found, this is where they'll be.

The demarcation between the perfectly manicured lawn of the golf club and the swath of natural wetland is stark. The ground below me is squelchy and brown. It is carpeted by plants that seem to grow horizontally; the saltworts and sandworts bred for saline waters. They're like tentacles emanating from some unseen body, spreading out in a bid to cover every sliver of ground and hold it firm against the marram grass. Pools permeate the soggy ground, and viscous streams have coiled their way up from the sea.

Deeper still are the trenches that seem to cut through the bog at random. It's as if a benevolent giant reached down and trailed its fingers through the mud, hollowing it out for nervous birds to hide in. From one of these clefts, the tangerine bill of a heron protrudes, attesting to the cleft's depth in concealing such a large creature.

Smaller birds share the marsh. A little egret, hunched over, looking like an animate plastic bag, strides away from me as I approach. A flock of linnets feasting on the ground rises amid a chorus of chirps, dwarfed by the dark bulk of a starling in their midst. Every time I stop to scan the surrounds with my binoculars, a redshank takes flight, mistaking my motionlessness for a sign of malevolent intent.

Suddenly, from towards the mainland, a merlin materialises out of thin air. Wings beating with purpose, she sweeps low over the marsh, causing pandemonium among the finches and starlings. They erupt in a mass panic. This is no murmuration, for the merlin has taken them by surprise and left them no time to co-ordinate their defence. Instead, they take off in a great mushrooming, trying to pull their pursuer in a thousand directions. But her focus is true as she twists and turns over the wet earth. I follow her and her quarry until they shrink into distant specs, the result of the chase uncertain.

Further out, the marsh gives way to a trough filled by the Irish Sea, dividing Bull Island from the mainland. The border is not definite but gradual, with islands of grass like fortresses beyond enemy lines moated by the sea. Here, the softer ground, less corrupted by marshy outgrowth, is ideal for the godwits that probe long, pink bills into the mud. Teal graze among them, semi-circles of flecked brown and grey scuttling along. On the water itself, a vast fleet of shelducks undulates with the waves. I'm excited to see among them the occasional, elegant form of a pintail, sleeker, with a chocolate head curving into a long white neck, the eponymous sharp tail held up proudly.

Just then, I'm startled by a small, streaky brown entity bursting from the marsh beneath me. Wings beating frantically, it gives two rasping barks as it swerves low over the bog, merging back into it as the bird alights just a few metres away.

In the rush, I struggle to catch sight of it in my binoculars. The size is hard to deduce, and the bill completely out of view. But to my delight, I can make out no white trailing edges to the wings: the standards of a common snipe in retreat. Jack snipe lack these entirely.

Being as well hidden as they so often are, the best way to tell the snipes apart is by the way they flush. Common snipe usually rise high, zigzagging away in uncoordinated panic. Jack snipe prefer to hug the ground as they escape, and feel less of a need to put great distance between you and them, confident that their cryptic feathering will hide them from harm.

It hugs the ground as I'd hoped. Whatever snipe this is, it's agonizingly close. But as I scan the patch I know it's landed in, there's no sign. No black holes for eyes, no head protruding. There and not there.

I determine to get closer, but one of the murky streams that bisect the marsh stands in my way. It's too thick to ford, and so I must content myself with studying the seemingly lifeless patch of bog from afar, hoping the jack snipe will relax enough to emerge.

It doesn't. Time and again I scope this thin patch of waterlogged grass from side to side, framed in the black of my binocular lenses. I know it's there; it hasn't taken flight since. And my frustration burns. There are no tall plants for the creature to crouch behind, no troughs in the mud to duck into. And yet its camouflage is so absolute that it remains hidden in plain sight.

I reflect on the jack snipe's scientific name: *Lymocryptes minimus*. *Minimus*: minimal, something small and illusory. *Cryptes* comes from *krypto*, meaning hidden. It is this word that lends its name to cryptozoology, the study of unknown animals, the yetis and Loch Ness Monsters of this world. It's a pseudo-science that's always fascinated me. I remain entranced by the notion that monsters could still lurk among us, in the shrinking pockets of unexplored space this world holds. In places where jungle still grows wild and free, and the undergrowth is so dense it obscures everything within a few feet of your face, carpeting valleys that rise and dip into each other all the way to the horizon. Who is to say what could not be hidden there?

But the jack snipe is as *krypto* as any cryptid, those hidden creatures that fixate cryptozoologists. This is no vast wilderness in which I stand, no lofty Himalayan peak forged in continental collisions, no forest with roots stretching back to antiquity. This is an island, barely five kilometres long, in the shadow of a thriving capital, raised from the sea only with the help of man. It does not feel like a place where hidden things should flourish. And the fact that the jack snipe does so makes me begrudge it with my respect as I decide to return to the mainland.

Given their elusiveness, some birders have developed a simple technique for finding jack snipe: wade through some suitable habitat in the hopes of flushing one out. But as I stare out at the vast expanse of swamp laid out before me, I concede that this is both practically unfeasible as well as poor form, frightening a bird into flight for the sake of a fleeting view. I've seen this tactic done with reed-dwelling rails in Canada. I won't replicate it here. I leave my quarry to forage in peace, a phantom abandoned to the bog. By now my feet are soaked through with marsh water, and the winter chill leaves them numb. The warmth of home beckons.

The jack snipe in absentia might have been keeping low, but as I approach the causeway once more, the rest of the flourishing birdlife Bull Island is known for is out in force. Godwits and teal busy themselves about different food sources on the shoreline. Grey plovers skulk among them, looking like juvenile gulls in their drab winter wear. Grassy knolls are bubble-wrapped in dunlins, beaks tucked in wings, leaving them little more than small grey lumps.

As the road progresses, the rising tide to the left creates a patchwork of gullies through the mire. Pintails, so rare on all the other wetlands I've frequented across Ireland, are plentiful here. Everywhere, the brackish water seems to be broken by the white streak of a male's neck and breast, crowned as always by the chocolate head. Those on land, waddling among the marsh greenery, are often kind enough to pause, motionless for my camera like dark-topped bowling pins, more caught in deep thought than frozen by fear. Watch them like this for long enough and your mind questions whether they are living at all, or hoaxes planted to mislead birders or illegal marksmen.

The pintails are more at home here in the no-man's land between solid ground and sea, a space they share with the herons, hunched over, dagger-like bills jutting out. But the open water calls for more assertive sorts. Here, the brent geese that had once clung together in twos and threes across the mudflats are now gathered in flocks of hundreds. They make a seething mass of honking flesh, riding the tide.

Scattered among them, the shelducks are silent, not needing sound to draw attention. Their feathers alone are enough to demand that. As they leisurely swim, their whites, pinks, russets and greens seem to bleed into the water. It's like a dozen artists, in a fit of despair, have cast the apparatus of their craft into the sea, leaving the waves to paint the waters of Dublin Bay.

And so it is, as I depart this wild oasis in the shadow of Ireland's capital, I'm enveloped in the sounds and colours of birds.

BIBLIOGRAPHY AND SOURCES

INTRODUCTION: A NATION AND ITS BIRDS

'Agriculture Policy and the Natural Environment', *Birdwatch Ireland*, https:// birdwatchireland.ie/our-work/advocacy-policy/agriculture-forestry/ [accessed 25 July 2019].

'Birds of conservation concern in Ireland 2014–2019', *Birdwatch Ireland*, https://birdwatchireland.ie/?fileticket=VcYOTGOjNbA%3D&tabid=178 [accessed 25 July 2019].

Murphy, Darragh, 'Ireland's native woodlands are quietly disappearing', *Irish Times*, 2018.

Orwell, George, *Essays* (Penguin Modern Classics, 2000).

'Seven meek and mighty animals from Ireland that are now extinct', *Irish Post*, 2016, https://www.irishpost.com/life-style/seven-meek-mighty-animals-ireland-now-extinct-107054 [accessed 25 July 2019].

MERLIN

Buchanan, Joseph B., 'Change in Merlin Hunting Behaviour Following Recovery of Peregrine Falcon Populations Suggests Mesopredator Suppression', *Journal of Raptor Research*, 2011.

Cresswell, Will, 'Song as a Pursuit-Deterrent Signal, and Its Occurrence Relative to Other Anti-Predation Behaviours of Skylark (*Alauda arvensis*) on Attack by Merlins (*Falco columbarius*)', *Behavioural Ecology and Sociobiology*, 1994.

D'Alton, John and J.R. O'Flanagan, *The History of Dundalk and Its Environs* (Hodges, Smith & Co., 1864).

Jones, Calvin, 'Merlin (*Falco columbarius*)', *Ireland's Wildlife*, https://www. irelandswildlife.com/merlin-falco-columbarius/ [accessed 25 July 2019].

King, Anthony, 'Flying high: Peregrine falcons return to Irish skies', *Irish Times*, 2018.

Lusby, John, 'Merlins in Ireland: getting to know our most elusive falcon', *Birdwatch Ireland*, https://www.birdwatchireland.ie/Publications/eWings/eWingsIssue77February2016/tabid/1501/Default.aspx [accessed 25 July 2019].

'Merlin: Life History', *The Cornell Lab of Ornithology*, https://www.allaboutbirds.org/guide/Merlin/lifehistory [accessed 25 July 2019].

'Merlin', *The Cornell Lab of Ornithology, Birds of North America*, https://birdsna.org/Species-Account/bna/species/merlin/introduction [accessed 25 July 2019].

Viney, Michael, 'Another Life: Location, location, location – the lives of peregrines', *Irish Times*, 2014.

GOOSANDER

'Bethada Náem nÉrenn', https://celt.ucc.ie/published/T201000G/text008.html [accessed 26 July 2019]

'Common Merganser', *The Cornell Lab of Ornithology, Birds of North America*, https://birdsna.org/Species-Account/bna/species/commer/introduction [accessed 25 July 2019].

Couzens, Dominic, 'Goosander', *Bird Watching* 2017.

Haggerty, Bridget, 'St. Kevin - founder of Glendalough', *Irish Culture & Customs*, https://www.irishcultureandcustoms.com/ASaints/Kevin.html [accessed 25 July 2019].

Hanson, Alan R. and Joseph J. Kerekes, 'Limnology and Aquatic Birds: Proceedings of the Fourth Conference Working Group on Aquatic Birds of Societas Internationalis Limnologiae (SIL), Sackville, New Brunswick, Canada, August 3–7, 2003', *Springer Science & Business Media*, 2009.

Kinsella, David, 'Exploring the Mining History of County Wicklow', *County Wicklow Heritage*, 2015, http://www.countywicklowheritage.org/page/the_glendalough_mines [accessed 25 July 2019].

Sanders, Georgia, 'Experiencing Ireland's Sacred Places – Glendalough', http://www.culturehoney.com/experiencing-irelands-sacred-places-glendalough/ [accessed 25 July 2019].

'Species Focus: Goosander', *Winter Wings* (Birdwatch Ireland, 2013).

'The Legend of St. Kevin and the Blackbird', *Luminarium.org*, http://www.luminarium.org/mythology/ireland/stkevin.htm [accessed 25 July 2019].

GREY PARTRIDGE

Abbot, Patrick, 'Ireland's Peat Bogs', *WesleyJohnston.com*, https://www.wesleyjohnston.com/users/ireland/geography/bogs.html [accessed 25 July 2019].

Beani, Laura and Francesco Dessì-Fulgheri, 'Mate choice in the grey partridge, *Perdix perdix*: role of physical and behavioural male traits', *Animal Behaviour* (1995).

'Bog Plants Book', *Irish Peatland Conservation Council*, http://www.ipcc.ie/discover-and-learn/resources/bog-plant-book/ [accessed 25 July 2019].

Bouglouan, Nicole, 'Grey Partridge', *Oiseaux-birds.com*, http://www.oiseaux-birds.com/card-grey-partridge.html [accessed 31 July 2019].

'Carnivorous Plants – Killers in the Bog', *Irish Peatland Conservation Council*, http://www.ipcc.ie/a-to-z-peatlands/carnivorous-plants-killers-in-the-bog/ [accessed 25 July 2019].

Collins, Richard, 'Partridges rare in Irish pear tree', *Irish Examiner*, 2009.

Downing, John, 'Contentious turf-cutting ban to be lifted for most bogs', *Irish Independent*, 2014.

Feehan, John and Grace O'Donovan, *The Bogs of Ireland: An Introduction to the Natural, Cultural and Industrial Heritage of Irish Peatlands* (University College, Dublin, Environmental Institute, 1996).

Gallagher, Rowan, 'Rise in illegal turf-cutting on protected bogs', *Irish Times*, 2012.

'Partridge Annual Lifecycle', *Greypartridge.ie*, https://www.greypartridge.ie/?page_id=46 [accessed 25 July 2019].

'Polish mates for our dying breed of partridge', *Irish Times*, 2000.

Thompson, Sylvia, 'Ireland's industrial heritage: the past you might not know we had', *Irish Times*, 2015.

Walsh, Anne Marie, 'Employment blow for midlands as Bord na Móna announces 430 job losses', *Irish Independent*, 2018.

Woodworth, Paddy, 'Grey partridge conservation takes flight in Co Dublin', *Irish Times*, 2015.

RED GROUSE

Bouglouan, Nicole, 'Red grouse', *Oiseaux-birds.com*, http://www.oiseaux-birds.com/card-red-grouse.html [accessed 25 July 2019].

Collins, Richard, 'The great grouse mystery', *Irish Examiner*, 2006.

Jackman, Nancy, *The Cook's Tale* (Coronet, 2012).

Kreilkamp, Vera, 'Country Houses and the Arts', *Encyclopaedia of Irish History and Culture* (2004).

Lawlor, Chris, 'From a spark to a firebrand: Feagh Mac Hugh O'Byrne', *History Ireland*, 2013.

Lydon, J.F., 'Medieval Wicklow – A Land of War', *Geography Publications*, 1994.

Medcalf, David, 'In step on the Military Road', *The Wicklow People*, 2017.

O'Toole, Lorcan and Mieke Muyllaert, 'Glenfarne Red Grouse Habitat Study and Management Proposals, Boleybrack Mountain, County Leitrim', Heritage Council, 2007.

'Old Military Road', *Visitwicklow.ie*, https://visitwicklow.ie/item/old-military-road/ [accessed 25 July 2019].

'Red Grouse conservation in Ireland', *Countryside Alliance*, https://countrysideallianceireland.org/environmental-rural/red-grouse-conservation-in-ireland/ [accessed 30 March 2018].

CORNCRAKE

Bouglouan, Nicole, 'Corncrake', *Oiseaux-birds.com*, 25 July 2019 [accessed 6 June 2018].

'Corncrakes continue to decline', *Birdwatch Ireland*, https://www.birdwatchireland.ie/Publications/eWings/eWingsIssue101February2018/Corncrakescontinuetodecline/tabid/1625/Default.aspx [accessed 25 July 2019].

'Corncrake Friendly Farming', *Rosewood Farm*, http://rosewood.farm/blog/4590880622/Corncrake-Friendly-Farming/11214535 [accessed 25 July 2019].

'Corn Crake', *WhatBird.com*, https://identify.whatbird.com/obj/1006/_/corn_crake.aspx [accessed 25 July 2019].

Deegan, Gordon, 'How Ireland's elusive corncrake has come back from the brink of extinction', *Irish Times*, 2019.

Dempsey, Eric and Michael O'Clery, *The Complete Guide to Ireland's Birds* (Gill & Macmillan, 2002).

Harrison Therman, Dorothy, *Stories From Tory Island* (Country House, 1998).

Robinson, Ann, 'The Sinking of HMS Wasp – A Mystery Veiled in Darkness', *Coastmonkey.ie*, http://coastmonkey.ie/hms-wasp-tory-island/ [accessed 25 July 2019].

CUCKOO

Collins, Richard, 'The Cuckoo: Ireland's Most Scandalous Bird!', *RTÉ*, https://www.rte.ie/radio/mooneygoeswild/fp2012/cuckoo.html [accessed 25 July 2019].

'Cuckoos impersonate hawks by matching their "outfits"', *Science Daily*, https://www.sciencedaily.com/releases/2013/10/131016112704.htm [accessed 31 July 2019].

Douglas, D.J.T., S.E. Newson, D.I. Leech, D.G. Noble, and R.A. Robinson, 'How important are climate-induced changes in host availability for population processes in an obligate brood parasite, the European Cuckoo?', *Oikos*, 2010.

Feeney, William, 'Egg colours make cuckoos masters of disguise', *The Conversation*, 2014, https://phys.org/news/2014-11-egg-colours-cuckoos-masters-disguise.html [accessed 25 July 2019].

Flegg, Jim, *Birds of the British Isles* (Black Cat, 1998).

Karikehalli, Shweta, 'Birds Inherited Colorful Eggs From Dinosaurs', *Audubon.org*, https://www.audubon.org/news/birds-inherited-colorful-eggs-dinosaurs [accessed 25 July 2019].

'Modern Birds Inherited Colored Eggs from Their Dinosaur Ancestors, Study Says', *Sci-news.com*, http://www.sci-news.com/paleontology/colored-dinosaur-eggs-06567.html [accessed 25 July 2019].

'No sign of the cuckoo', *Irish Examiner*, 2015.

Switek, Brian, 'Baby Dinosaur Mystery', *Smithsonian.com*, https://www.smithsonianmag.com/science-nature/baby-dinosaur-mystery-4610005/ [accessed 25 July 2019].

'Who were the Black Irish?', *Ireland-information.com*, http://www.ireland-information.com/articles/blackirish.htm [accessed 25 July 2019].

'Why some cuckoos have blue eggs', *Science Daily*, https://www.sciencedaily.com/releases/2016/01/160121121514.htm [accessed 25 July 2019].

Yong, Ed, 'Cuckoos mimic hawks to fool small birds', *National Geographic*, 2008.

GREAT SKUA

Bayes, J.C., M.J. Dawson and G.R. Potts 'The food and feeding behaviour of the Great Skua in the Faroes', *Bird Study*, 2009.

Canning, Joe, 'The Miscreant of Mayo', *stairnaheireann.net*, https://stairnaheireann.net/tag/the-miscreant-of-mayo-joe-canning-2014-all-rights-reserved/ [accessed 25 July 2019].

Couzens, Dominic, 'Great skua: beauty and the beast', *BBC Wildlife*, 2010.

Duff, Chris, *On Celtic Tides: One Man's Journey Around Ireland by Sea Kayak* (St. Martin's Griffin, 2004).

Furness, Robert W., *The Skuas* (Poyser, 2010).

'Mayo's islands are offshore jewels', *The Mayo News*, 2012.

McDermott, Niamh, 'History of the Irish Currach', *Ouririshheritage.org*, https://www.ouririshheritage.org/content/archive/topics/st_josephs_secondary_school_castlebar_co_mayo/history_of_the_irish_currach [accessed 25 July 2019].

Thompson, Laura, *A Different Class of Murder: The Story of Lord Lucan* (Apollo, 2018).

RING OUZEL

'Bartholomew Colles Watkins, Landscape Painter – Irish Artists', *LibraryIreland.com*, https://www.libraryireland.com/irishartists/bartholomew-colles-watkins.php [accessed 25 July 2019].

Bouglouan, Nicole, 'Ring Ouzel', *Oiseaux-birds.com*, http://www.oiseaux-birds.com/card-ring-ouzel.html [accessed 25 July 2019].

Coghlan, Pete, 'Famous Places', *Beaufort Parish*, https://www.beaufort-parish.com/famous-places/ [accessed 25 July 2019].

Hillis, Paul, 'Ireland's rare breeding birds', *Birdwatch Ireland*, https://www.birdwatchireland.ie/Publications/eWings/eWingsIssue23August2011/IrelandsRareBreedingBirds/tabid/1197/Default.aspx [accessed 25 July 2019].

'Mick Green on Ring Ouzel Research', *Films for Ecology*, https://www.youtube.com/watch?v=8oe2v-N3ggI, [accessed 25 July 2019].

'The Evolution of Birds: How Adaptation Works', *RSPB.org.uk*, https://www.rspb.org.uk/birds-and-wildlife/natures-home-magazine/birds-and-wildlife-articles/how-do-birds-survive/how-adaptation-works/ [accessed 25 July 2019].

BARN OWL

Anderson, Glynn, *Birds of Ireland: Facts, Folklore & History* (The Collins Press, 2008).

Bachmann, Thomas, S. Blazek, T. Erlinghagen, W. Baumgartner, and H. Wagner, 'Barn Owl Flight', *Nature-Inspired Fluid Mechanics*, 2012.

'Don't let the barn owl become a late, late species', *Irish Times*, 2007.

Ferriter, Diarmaid, 'The FitzGeralds of Carton House – a deeply dysfunctional family: The Decline and Fall of the Dukes of Leinster', *Irish Times*, 2014.

Flegg, Jim (1998), *Birds of the British Isles* (Black Cat, 1998)

Knudsen, Eric I., 'The Hearing of the Barn Owl', *Scientific American*, 1981.

Konishi, Masakazu, 'How the Owl Tracks Its Prey', *Scientific American*, 1973.

Smal, C.M., 'The diet of the Barn Owl *Tyto alba* in southern Ireland, with reference to a recently introduced prey species— the Bank Vole *Clethrionomys glareolus*', *Bird Study*, 1987.

Viney, Michael, 'Has the dwindling barn owl had a shrew too many?', *Irish Times*, 2012.

JAY

Balter, Michael, 'Meet the Bird Brainiacs: Eurasian Jay', *Audubon*, 2016.

Cheke, Lucy G., Christopher D. Bird and Nicola S. Clayton, 'Tool-use and instrumental learning in the Eurasian Jay', *Animal Cognition*, 2011, Vol. 3, Issue 14.

Dakota, Aqua Nara, 'Garrulus glandarius Eurasian jay', *Animal Diversity Web*, https://animaldiversity.org/accounts/Garrulus_glandarius/ [accessed 25 July 2019].

Foulds, Kathy, 'The Creation of a Thousand Forests is in One Acorn', *Fotahouse.com*, http://fotahouse.com/my-oak-tree-for-hundreds-of-years-will-live/ [accessed 25 July 2019].

Hickey, Donal, 'Ireland has great woodland but has the lowest forest cover of all European countries', *Irish Examiner*, 2016.

'History of Forestry in Ireland', *Teagasc.com*, https://www.teagasc.ie/crops/forestry/advice/general-topics/history-of-forestry-in-ireland/ [accessed 25 July 2019].

'J is for Jay', Cambridge University, https://www.youtube.com/watch?v=KWEkY2Fo3kQ&t=187s [accessed 01 August 2019].

Prendeville, Tom, 'The Secret History of the Phoenix Park', *Irish Independent*, 2014.

HEN HARRIER

Birdwatch Ireland, 'The bird behind the headlines: getting to know the Hen Harrier', *eWings*, 2015.

Dempsey, Eric and Michael O'Clery, *Finding Birds in Ireland, The Complete Guide, 2nd Edition* (Gill & Macmillan, 2014).

Gittings, Tom, Tom Kelly, John O'Halloran, Josephine Pithon and Mark Wilson, 'The distribution of Hen Harriers in Ireland in relation to land use cover, particularly forest cover', *COFORD Connects*, 2006.

'Hen Harriers', *Clive Muirshiel Regional Park*, http://clydemuirshiel.co.uk/guide/hen-harriers/ [accessed 25 July 2019].

'Hen Harrier Conservation and the Forestry Sector in Ireland', *National Parks & Wildlife Service*, 2015, https://www.npws.ie/sites/default/files/publications/pdf/HHTRP%20-%20Forestry%20-%20V3.2.pdf [accessed 25July 2019].

'Hen Harrier foodpass', RSPB Videos, https://www.youtube.com/watch?v=KH2ZE3uuuzg [accessed 01 August 2019].

'Hen/Northern Harrier', *The Cornell Lab of Ornithology, Birds of North America*, https://birdsna.org/Species-Account/bna/species/norhar/introduction [accessed 25 July 2019].

'Hen Harrier Skydance', RSPB Video, https://www.youtube.com/watch?v=cbuovJyIWLs [accessed 01 August 2019].

Lehane, Dennis, 'Scheme can enable upland farmers and the hen harrier to thrive together', *Irish Examiner*, 2018.

Lewis, Amy, 'Why planting trees could be bad for Ireland's hen harriers', *Irish Times*, 2018.

Nugent, Louise, 'In search of a cure: the pilgrimage of James Shee to Lady's Island, Co. Wexford in 1694', *Pilgrimage in Medieval Ireland*, https://pilgrimagemedievalireland.com/2013/09/11/in-search-of-a-cure-the-pilgrimage-of-james-shee-to-ladys-island-co-wexford-in-1694/ [accessed 25 July 2019].

'Our Lady's Island, County Wexford', *Holy Well*, http://irelandsholywells.blogspot.com/2012/03/our-ladys-island-county-wexford.html [accessed 25 July 2019].

Purcell Bates, Stella , 'Our Lady's Island History', *Historical Wexford*, 2016, https://www.facebook.com/HiddenGemsofCarne/posts/brilliant-post-about-the-history-of-ladys-island-worth-a-read/1781989542020220/ [accessed 25 July 2019].

Reiner, Bill, 'Texas Naturalist's Notes By Bill Reiner', *Travis Audubon*, https://travisaudubon.org/uncategorized/texas-naturalists-notes-by-bill-reiner-4 [accessed 25 July 2019].

Shiels, Daniel, 'Column: Yola and Fingalian – the forgotten ancient English dialects of Ireland', *TheJournal.ie*, https://www.thejournal.ie/readme/column-yola-and-fingalian-%E2%80%93-the-forgotten-ancient-english-dialects-of-ireland-985649-Jul2013/ [accessed 25 July 2019].

'The Skydancer: Hen Harriers in Ireland', *Birdwatch Ireland*, https://www.birdwatchireland.ie/OurWork/PolicyAdvocacy/IrelandsSkydancer/tabid/1499/Default.aspx [accessed 25 July 2019].

Warner, Dick, 'When is the last time you saw a hen harrier?', *Irish Examiner*, 2017.

Woodworth, Paddy, 'Can we keep the hen harrier dancing in Irish skies?', *Irish Times*, 2017.

JACK SNIPE

Appleton, Graham, 'Snipe & Jack Snipe in the UK and Ireland', *Wadertales*, https://wadertales.wordpress.com/2016/09/20/snipe-jack-snipe-in-the-united-kingdom/ [accessed 26 July 2019].

Bouglouan, Nicole, 'Jack Snipe', *Oiseaux-birds.com*, http://www.oiseaux-birds.com/card-jack-snipe.html [accessed 26 July 2019].

'BTO Bird ID – Common and Jack Snipe', BTOvideo, https://www.youtube.com/watch?v=nYLOQv-uwOw [accessed 26 July 2019].

Oram, Hugh, 'An Irishman's Diary', *Irish Times*, 2006.

Woodworth, Paddy, 'Dublin's accidental island', *Irish Times*, 2012.